A Book of Days

Something Different

Steve Moore

There is something different here.
Deep hope, confusion.
Nothing clear, but the night and the star.
A child born as all of us,
yet with pains of arrival as never before,
and signs that hint of more.

Leaders come and go and speak of hope,
and promises of change, for others of course,
not for you and me, whose comfort must come first, as it should be.

Yet this one newborn will be so different.
He will ask hard questions and disturb our comfort and place.
He will call us down uncertain paths,
not well worn or familiar.
An invitation to lose yourself, and find your way.
As if to say we're made for more than
stumbling pride or grasping gain.
A wellspring that overflows, a joy,
that defies restraint or pain.

All from one who seems so small,
so out of place in stables and mangers,
and now ten thousand days and a life to go.

A Book of Days

Christmas Reflections from the Northwest

seedbed
PUBLISHING

Printed in the United States of America
ISBN: 978-1-62824-147-1

Library of Congress Control Number: 2014947514

Cover and page design by Brushfire Design Studio

SEEDBED PUBLISHING
Franklin, Tennessee
Seedbed.com
Sowing for a Great Awakening

This book is dedicated to the leaders, volunteers, board members, donors, workers, constituencies, and friends of nonprofit organizations in the Pacific Northwest who are "weaving the fabric of a healthy and verdant culture."

Contents

Acknowledgments

Gratitude is happiness doubled by wonder.
—G. K. Chesterton

Until one starts to write an acknowledgments page, one cannot fully realize how difficult it is to limit the sense of gratitude and wonder that fills such a project as this.

We would first like to thank Claire Sarah Smith, our extraordinary, gifted, patient, and persistent intern/fellow, who "herded" all of us in a skillful way that must bring pride to her native Texas. Every person involved with this project was blessed by Claire, and we are all deeply appreciative of the way she demonstrated a wisdom beyond her years.

We would also like to thank Stefanie Narhi, who not only supported and encouraged Claire, Father Rick, and Steve, but who also proofed, edited, typed, made suggestions, and gracefully kept many other pieces of the project on track.

Our friends at Seedbed Publishing were also such great partners, in particular Andrew Miller and J. D. Walt, along with Nick Perreault, Maren Kurek, Renee Chavez, and Holly Jones, who helped the project come together. You don't get a project like this done without faithful, committed, and gifted people who believe in what they are doing, and in what you are doing.

Of course, all of the contributors and those who have supported them are the heart of the project. One can imagine how challenging it is to just dip into the deep talent pool of leadership in the faith-based nonprofit world of the Pacific Northwest. In many ways, these contributing writers, most of whom are leaders, not only represent their organization or institution but also their peers and colleagues at the hundreds of other organizations who are a part of the vibrant region in which we serve. We all recognize we are part of something much bigger than ourselves.

I, Steve, would also like to give thanks for my parents, Wilford and Marian Moore, who gave me the love and spirit of Christmas. My children, Madison, Maegan, and Mollie, who have brought us joy and wonder every Christmas, and my wife, Thanne, who is the most remarkable companion for whom one could ever hope.

I, Rick, would like to thank my parents, Dr. Dick and Mrs. Doris Ganz, who established and kept in our household certain unbreakable traditions around the season of Advent and of Christmastide, but whose commitment to maintaining a personal relationship with Jesus over the years taught us six children what it looks like for God to come incarnately into the world and to transform it. I also express deepest admiration for the life of Saint Ignatius of Loyola (1492–1556), and the price he was willing to pay to live it—"For it is not much knowledge that fills and satisfies the soul, but the intimate understanding and relish of the truth."

Last and first, we want to express gratitude to Lyn and Karin Swanson, John and Sarah Castles, and Jeff and Sandy Grubb for their support, encouragement, and friendship. Lyn, John, and Jeff serve as the trustees of the M. J. Murdock Charitable Trust and seek to fulfill the mission "to nurture and enrich the spiritual, educational, cultural, and social life of individuals, families, and communities." They serve in this role with grace, wisdom, faithfulness, and steadfastness—traits that are mentioned over and over in *A Book of Days* and in every Christmas season. Along with the staff of the Murdock Trust, they regularly offer common grace for the common good. For all others, we give thanks; forgive our lack of space and thought to mention you here! May the thoughts expressed herein inspire, encourage, enlarge, and fill your Christmas season.

Introduction

STEVE MOORE

Advent is an ancient tradition and practice. It's a celebration that guides us in and through the Christmas season. Advent is a tradition that dates back hundreds of years to the very earliest Christians gathering to worship. It is a practice that can be found in cities, villages, towns, and locations all around the world. There are mentions of Advent as early in the life of the church as AD 275. It was an important practice of the early Christians in telling the stories and identifying the events and the people who were a part of the most amazing story ever told—the story of Jesus' birth, Christmas.

Advent is important for us in the twenty-first century because it invites us to establish a new rhythm to our lives, to recalibrate our lives and our living to a kingdom rhythm, one that will serve us during all of our year. Though there are varying practices around the weeks of Advent, most include emphasizing some of the main parts of the story of Christmas as told in the four Gospels, we light a Prophecy Candle to bring to mind that Jesus' coming had been promised and prophesied for generations before Christ's birth, calling all of humankind to "preparc the way for the Lord" (Isa. 40:3). Jesus coming into the world was part of a much older story of God's love and desire for redemption of humankind that goes back to Genesis, the beginning.

On the second Sunday of Advent, we light a candle that introduces a week to reflect on Bethlehem—this out-of-the-way, very unusual place where Christ's birth took place. It reminds us that "place" matters—that God cares about where you and I live and that there are no insignificant people or places.

In the third week, we light a candle to remind us of the angels—and that Jesus' birth had cosmic implications, not just earthly ones! Angels appear, proclaim, comfort, announce, and call us to pay attention. Something unusual is happening that continually tells us, *Don't be afraid! There is good news!* God's promises are fulfilled this day with the birth of a baby. How could that be?

On the fourth week, our attention is directed to the shepherds and the wise men. They are unexpected and yet very important participants as the world's greatest event unfolds. They too have a special part that has shaped the story. Their stories help make our stories matter and help us see that something big is happening—God is taking on human flesh and living in our world.

The signature day of Advent, of course, is Christmas Day and is marked by lighting a candle in the center of the other four. Christmas Day is the pivotal day of the Christmas season. It helps focus our blurry world; it helps center our shakiness. But there is more to come.

What many Christians fail to realize is that the Christmas season is more than one day or the four weeks leading up to Christmas or the days after Christmas. Many of us have sung about the twelve days of Christmas but didn't realize that the fullness of the Christmas season includes the twelve days after Christmas! We have included further readings and reflections to guide these days and to lead us well into the New Year. All through Christmas, we are invited to allow incarnation—the miracle that the Christmas message brings—to be true in our lives in this special time and in all the ordinary days of our year.

May this Book of Days inspire, encourage, and enlarge your Christmas season and guide your journey of faith and the celebration of the birth of Christ. O come, let us adore him!

Steve Moore of the M. J. Murdock Charitable Trust lives in Portland, Oregon, with his wife, Thanne.

First Week of Advent

First Sunday of Advent

FR. RICK GANZ

ZECHARIAH 9:9–10 · ROMANS 13:11–14

And do this, understanding the present time: The hour has already come for you to wake up from your slumber, because our salvation is nearer now than when we first believed.
ROMANS 13:11

It Is Time

When Saint Paul wrote here that you need to "[understand] the present time" and "the hour has already come" and then "nearer now," he is not referring to clock-time. He means another kind of time. Saint Paul is talking about special times such as Advent or Christmastide that have special meaning and purpose. Such time is closer to the idea of "ripeness" than to that of minutes or months.

Consider the *ripeness* characteristic of this other kind of time. We, for example, decide to embrace someone beloved to us—we just know that it is the right time for it—it never occurs to us to determine how many seconds or minutes we ought to set aside for this gesture of friendship. We sense and then submit to follow an internal experience of timeliness. Saint Paul was adverting to this in his quotation above "the hour has already come . . . now." Advent is about such time.

Consider further the *fullness* (rather than *length*) characteristic of this other kind of time. We know what it is like when we spend time with a best friend, or listen to beautiful music, or walk carefree and with all senses alert in the wilderness. Time feels timeless, and rich, and thick. Nothing is taken from us; rather, we feel given much—"out of his fullness we have all received grace in place of grace already given" (John 1:16). Afterward, we wonder why we so rarely allot clock and calendar time for such full time to happen. Saint Paul wrote: "our salvation is nearer now than when we first believed." Advent is about such time.

This other kind of ripe and full time we experience as internal nudges, through which we feel directed to act. We feel the fittingness and timeliness that something happen, and now. By our willingness to follow such nudges, putting them to the test, learning how they work, some for good ends and others for ill, we grow in our ability to be led by the Spirit, to be taught by God. Advent and Christmas season are for such time.

But now we must become more *awake* than we are used to being—"to wake up from your slumber," as Saint Paul wrote. And such awakening includes our repentance for the many times that we have hidden in clock-time from God and from the exigency of this other kind of ripe-time, avoiding what we already know is fitting and timely for us to do *now*—"Yes," we say, "but not yet, please."

Remember how the Advent scriptures cry out to us to repent. This command comes from outside of us, in, for example, the voice of John the Baptist, or in our text, from Saint Paul. Yet the point lies not in the command to repent given us from outside ourselves; rather, the point of that command is about getting us to notice how fitting it would be (is it not so?), and timely (right?), for us to repent. We are nudged to notice, and so we may, and so we might choose . . . now. It is time. Right?

Dearest Lord, awaken us to how you prompt us in the fullness of time to act, and increase our capacity to discern your nudges and promptings, and to act on them with nimbleness and generosity. Amen.

Fr. Rick Ganz, SJ, has been a Jesuit and Roman Catholic priest for forty years, and is a teacher, writer, and spiritual director residing in Portland, Oregon.

First Monday of Advent

ROD WILSON

JEREMIAH 23:5–6 · 1 CORINTHIANS 1:4–9

"The days are coming," declares the Lord, "when I will raise up for David a righteous Branch, a King who will reign wisely and do what is just and right in the land. In his days Judah will be saved and Israel will live in safety. This is the name by which he will be called: The Lord Our Righteous Savior."
JEREMIAH 23:5–6

Eager Waiting, the Ultimate Oxymoron

Incredulous is probably the best word to describe the telephone solicitor's reaction when in response to his question, "Wouldn't you like to pay a little more in order to increase your Internet speed?" I said, "No. I am very happy with my Internet speed. It is not that long a wait." In a culture of quick, instant gratification, fast food, immediate communication, and the like, comfort with waiting seems counterintuitive, illogical, and bordering on wrong. Being happy to wait?

Advent begs the same question and similar reactions. Finding its etymological root in the Latin word *adventus*, or "coming," this is the season where we wait with eager expectancy. We adopt a posture that reflects faith; faith that what you are hoping for will come to be. We embrace a mind-set that reflects the unseen, a sense that what you cannot see now will eventually be visible. We invoke the ultimate oxymoron, eager waiting.

No doubt those who heard the Old Testament prophets had to adopt, embrace, and invoke this kind of sensibility. When Jeremiah told his hearers that "the days are coming" this was not his only citation of this phrase. Over and over again this was the phrase that God wanted to speak to his people. They could expect the Lord, the righteous Savior, to come as the Branch, the final King in the Davidic line. Wisdom, justice, righteousness, and safety would ensue. And so with the promise that these days were coming, God's people lived in faith, fixed their eyes on the unseen, and waited eagerly for the coming of the Messiah, the one who would bring the peace for which they hoped.

A similar message was given by the apostle Paul to the Corinthian church (see 1 Corinthians 1:4–9). In spite of their divisions and immorality, qualities that reflect a life in opposition to who Jesus is, he thanked God for the grace that was given to them. He assured them that, just as they had been called into the fellowship of Christ, they would be kept firm to the end, not because of their inherent goodness, but because of the faithfulness of God. In the interim, between their calling and the consummation, they would eagerly wait for the second coming of our Lord Jesus Christ. Again God's people are waiting, a statement that both describes spiritual reality but is also an invitation to a particular kind of lifestyle.

Waiting in a culture wired for speed often looks like toe-tapping, pulse-increasing impatience, with a dose of irritation and exasperation. Waiting in a culture tapped into the kingdom invites us to join with God's people of the Old Testament who longed for the days when the Messiah would come as the culmination of everything they anticipated. It also invites us to join with the church at Corinth in our recognition that in spite of all the frailty, brokenness, and sin in the church and the culture, we eagerly await the consummation of all things, the return of our Lord Jesus Christ.

Father, I come before you today deeply aware that I am living in, and frequently influenced by, the culture of speed. I find so much of my life is characterized by going quickly, and I confess before you that activity is more typical of my life than serenity. At the beginning of this Advent season, I pray that you will give me the faith to live my life connected to the kingdom and its values. I pray that you will help me to live here at this time and in this place infused by your grace as I eagerly await the second coming of the Lord Jesus Christ. I pray this in his name. Amen.

Dr. Rod Wilson is the president and a professor of counseling and psychology at Regent College and lives in Burnaby, Canada.

First Tuesday of Advent

BRUCE MCNICOL

ISAIAH 11:1–10 · COLOSSIANS 3:12

Therefore, as God's chosen people, holy and dearly loved . . .
COLOSSIANS 3:12

Enjoy the Chocolate!

A saint is "a person who is officially recognized by the Christian church as being very holy because of the way he or she *lived*," according to Merriam-Webster. *Wikipedia* defines a saint as "a person acknowledged as holy or virtuous, and typically regarded as being in heaven *after death*." Want to be a saint? Live holier than most. Then die. And perhaps we'll acknowledge you.

In contrast, read this biblical paragraph that guides the thoughts for the day and you'll discover God saying, as he does in several other scriptures, "[You are] holy." Now. Present tense. Wouldn't this be amazing? If only God were right!

Why are we convinced that we must wait for the afterlife to be holy, when the New Testament teaches us that we are made holy by him who loved us . . . to the end? At one level, the answer is pretty simple. We often drift to moralism or religious formulas.

More right behavior plus less wrong behavior equals holiness. But since we always feel as if we are short in some part of the *formula*, we never become holy. We live agonizingly and continually in a deficit position, until we die. This is not good news; in fact it can be a religious burden.

So, which is true? Are you a saint (a holy person) who sins? Or, are you a sinner, still striving to become a saint (a holy person)?

Advent is a season that challenges us to consider, in whom do you trust? *Wiki* or God? Yourself or your Creator? Suppose you trust who God says you are. If you do, the rest of Colossians 3:12–17 will burst open with scintillating flavors. You will realize this is not a list of to-dos so you can change yourself into somebody you are not. Rather, it is a list of qualities that express who you are, a saint. This is *how you mature into who you already are*, a saint. And this, my friends, is really good news! In fact, it is the good news of Christmas!

Therefore, living with compassion, kindness, humility, gentleness, patience, forgiveness, peace, and gratitude—which collectively are all expressions of love—is simply what saints do. Saints already have the DNA of Christ, which is a heart full of love. This is why God's commands are not burdensome. This is why Christ's burden is light. These are not qualities you have to work to cultivate, but *expressions* of who you are. Not a list of what you ought to *do*, but a list of what you *get* to do, because you own a new identity. Holiness, we are reminded, is not in what we do, can do, or should do; it lies in the startling truth of who loved us first . . . and last! It is who we are in Christ.

To a saint, the list of love in Colossians 3:12–17 is like saying, "Eat more chocolate!" So this Christmas, every time you see chocolate, be reminded of the gifts that are in you! This Advent season, celebrate who you are! Relax, and live out of who you are. Enjoy the chocolate!

Father, thank you for making me a saint now. I realize that I am a saint who sins, but I am no longer a sinner striving to become a saint. I know the Spirit can only live in me because you have made me holy by your work, not mine. Thank you for allowing me to love others now, through all these qualities in Colossians 3:12–17, because you have already given me a heart of love. I am free. I am grateful.

Dr. Bruce McNicol is the president of Truefaced and lives in Phoenix, Arizona.

First Wednesday of Advent

Ty Saltzgiver

PSALM 28:7–10 · JOHN 1:1–5

In the beginning was the Word, and the Word was with God, and the Word was God. He was with God in the beginning.
John 1:1–2

The Word Became Flesh

The disciple whom Jesus loved (whom we know as John) began his gospel with, "In the beginning was *the Word . . . the Word* was God. . . . He [the Word] was with God in the beginning" (italics mine). Matthew recorded the names for God's Son as Immanuel (God with us) and then as Jesus (the One who saves). John the Baptist called him "the Lamb of God, who takes away the sin of the world" (John 1:29). Those names are familiar to us. But calling Jesus "the Word" may not be as clear to us.

In Greek culture, the *logos* (word) was known as the foundational idea of all things known. John applies this idea to God in person; in other words, the idea becomes reality in a living, breathing person!

Does God stoop so low to become a real person? In many parts of the world, this is a shocking idea. Christianity says that God shows his greatness by being willing to do so.

And if the "Word became flesh" is not shocking enough, John goes on to suggest that Jesus is present with the Father in the creation of all things. Challenging ideas for sure, but what does all this mean to us?

Certainly by one's audible words a person's thoughts are made known. All of us want to know what God is like and what God thinks. Jesus, God's Word, reveals God to us. Otherwise, we'd only know him as almighty, infinite, the One who hung the stars, omni-everything.

We wonder at times, *Does God know me, understand me, know what I'm going through, get what I feel?* Well, Jesus does know something about the world, about depth, meaning, and hope because he was there when it all started. Then, he entered into that world and experienced all of life as we have, so yes, he knows us. But more than that, he took on flesh and experienced life as we do.

We can also release our striving to reach or please God, and receive the wonder and wonderful good news of Christmas. God is seeking us—a caring God drawing close to us. Humans try to figure out God. Wondrously and happily, we have God revealing himself to us. The Word became flesh and dwelt among us.

God, in this season of waiting and anticipation,
give us eyes to see you actively seeking us. Help us to
recognize your willingness to come be among us and
embrace your gift of yourself in this Advent season.
Amen.

Ty Saltzgiver is the senior vice president of the Midwest Division for Young Life, residing in Colorado Springs, Colorado.

First Thursday of Advent

Daniel J. Martin

PSALM 92:1–4 · ROMANS 3:21–26

But now apart from the law the righteousness of God has been made known, to which the Law and the Prophets testify.
Romans 3:21

God's Good Work

We have all been burdened by the weight of sin—whether our own, someone close to us, or by seeing the devastation that seems to reign in the world at times. We have made mistakes, broken promises, hurt those we love, and have had to ask for forgiveness. We all understand the chaos and confusion that sin produces in the world, and we know all too well our inability to choose the right thing, even when we want to. We fall short each and every day. The glory of the gospel is that we don't have to live under the weight of sin any longer, entirely because of the mercy of our Savior.

Saint Paul taught that the law was given in the Old Testament to expose our sin. However, in the person of Christ, we have been given far more than just that. In his coming, he fulfilled the law and ushered in a new kingdom—a kingdom fueled by the grace, justice, mercy, and by the righteousness of a loving God, who freed us from our sin, establishing us in his own righteousness. What is left to us is to embody this faith in Christ, in order not only to deepen in us this gift of righteousness, but also to help God usher in the kingdom begun in the work of Christ.

Furthermore, through Christ's life and sacrifice, we are given assurance concerning the character of God. Despite the brokenness that is present in the world, we know that we serve a God whose faithfulness is real and enduring, and whose promises can be trusted. And all of this is true in spite of our sinfulness. As one commentator has said, this righteousness that we have been given "originates in God's mind, is motivated by God's character, and is 'purchased' by God's work in Christ."[1]

God's gracious gifts to us, and to all, deserve our insightful and unceasing praise. The psalmist spoke well when he exclaimed in Psalm 92:1–4:

It is good to praise the Lord
  and make music to your name, O Most High,
proclaiming your love in the morning
  and your faithfulness at night,
to the music of the ten-stringed lyre
  and the melody of the harp.
For you make me glad by your deeds, Lord;
  I sing for joy at what your hands have done.

Our gracious Father, may we never cease singing for joy and thankfulness at the righteousness that has been given to us as a gift through the sacrifice of your only Son. We desire a deeper faith that results from dependence upon you, and upon you alone. We pray for a deepened experience of your Spirit, so that our faith emboldens us to act for your glory. Amen.

Dr. Daniel J. Martin is the president of Seattle Pacific University, living in Seattle, Washington.

First Friday of Advent

PHIL ROGERS

PSALMS 72:1–7 · ROMANS 5:1

Therefore, since we have been justified through faith, we have peace with God through our Lord Jesus Christ.
ROMANS 5:1

Practicing Peace

The Advent season provides an opportunity to slow down mentally and spiritually, to reflect back and to look forward, and to be re-centered in the practice of greater spiritual alertness, while committing ourselves to expectant waiting.

I found myself waiting expectantly recently, when I sat in my car at the Boise, Idaho, airport. It is not my custom to wait at airports randomly wondering whether any friends of mine will magically appear. One time I knew when a friend was to arrive, and so for weeks in advance he and I coordinated our plan for me to be there to pick him up, and on time. His text to me, sent from his plane on the departing runway, confirmed that I would be meeting him at the baggage claim area ninety minutes later. For this reason, I turned down that day a gracious offer to spend the day skiing, and instead had a day given over to expecting his arrival. But awaiting expectantly for something, or for someone, is in a certain sense to experience it as already present.

Saint Paul wrote, "Therefore, since we have been justified through faith, we have peace with God through our Lord Jesus Christ." Through the gift of faith, God's peace is a gift already given us, established by an event that has already taken place. The plane of peace, if you will, has already taken off and landed in the person and work of Jesus Christ. However, learning how to meet and to welcome that peace into our hearts, and to live out of it, takes practice.

Peace begins by remembering and embracing what has already been done for us, and living out of that peace-filled center. Theologian Karl Barth put it well: "Peace is the proper ordering of the relation between [ourselves as ourselves] with God as God."[2] In other words, worry and fear are the result of forgetting God at the airport—an unnecessary concern of many things (see Matthew 6:25–34) instead of the freedom of our-God-for-us reality. When we don't remember the true state of things, we are likely to leave God's peace at the curb. Expectantly waiting for Jesus during Advent is an opportunity for us to remember what he has already done, and to practice living more deeply from the completed work of his grace.

Expectant waiting is an active process of putting faith into practice. In my opening example, I chose to clear my schedule so that I could drive to the airport and joyfully await and welcome my friend.

All practice works this way. We learn to hit a baseball in a batting cage. We dance in front of a mirror before we dare step onto a stage. We do our math on a whiteboard before we build a bridge. So, too, we must practice abiding in God's peace when the heat is off, so that we can practice peace when the heat is on.

From his jail cell the apostle Paul told the church in Philippi: "I have learned the secret of being content" (Phil. 4:12). He already had peace when he needed it. Peace becomes a learned state of the heart and mind, our praxis, born of active practice.

We have peace (and he has us) when we practice peace. And we have more peace the more we practice. It is no surprise when the plane lands. We can say, "It's good to see you, friend." Advent is coming. Peace is here.

Dear Lord, grant us the discipline and faith
today to practice peace in our uncertain lives.
Thank you for giving us the tools to practice
peace through your faithfulness and love.

Dr. Phil Rogers is campus minister, associate dean of students, and professor of New Testament and Christian spirituality at the College of Idaho in Caldwell, Idaho.

First Saturday of Advent

DAVID ALEXANDER

ZECHARIAH 9:9–12 · MATTHEW 25: 1–13

"But while they were on their way to buy the oil, the bridegroom arrived. The virgins who were ready went in with him to the wedding banquet. And the door was shut. Later the others also came. 'Lord, Lord,' they said, 'open the door for us!' But he replied, 'Truly I tell you, I don't know you.' Therefore keep watch, because you do not know the day or the hour."
MATTHEW 25:10–13

The Fullness of Time

The people of Israel had waited! They waited for so long that they almost gave up. In fact, judging by the way they lived their lives, generation upon generation had given up. They felt God forsaken. The promised one, whatever the promise, was not coming—at least it seemed.

Then, finally, in what Paul later called "the fullness of time," he came. Yet his coming was so other-than-expected that those who waited missed his arrival. They were looking for a conquering ruler. Instead, God's angel choir announced the arrival of a baby to a hillside congregation of humble, hardworking people—hardly the way to launch a plan to establish a kingdom that would change the world.

Today, we remember their waiting, their hunger, their hopelessness, their hurt. We remember the arrival of the baby-Savior-in-waiting. This time of remembering is called

Advent. Jesus came and lived among us, and we beheld his glory, full of grace and truth.

Now he is gone. He promised he would return. But he's gone. And once again, we wait.

While he was here, he told us stories, parables. Some of them were insights on waiting. Proper waiting. The parable of the ten virgins is such a story, waiting that has a worthwhile result coming. Waiting based on substance—not wishful thinking.

Disciples of Jesus, citizens of the kingdom of God, do not wait without hope. This time the waiting is different. He was clear in what to expect and what to do. The Bridegroom will come, but he will not come on a timetable that is published. Now is not the time to go to a hilltop and await his return; now is the time to roll up your sleeves and practice the art of fully living in the present and all the while—stay prepared.

While he is away we are called to prepare for his return. Five bridesmaids did. Five did not. The trappings of readiness aren't enough; there needs to be fuel to fire our readiness. To be ready for the coming of the Bridegroom, to be welcomed into the wedding banquet, we must take action. What is the fuel for your readiness?

Jesus told this story to both encourage us and warn us. It's as if he said, "While I am away, be about my business. I will return, and when I do, only those who are actively, faithfully living out their desire to be part of my marriage feast will be welcome."

What does he expect of us while we wait? To care for and invite the humble, broken, hardworking people of the land to come join in changing the kingdom of this world into the kingdom of our Lord—do that, and you're ready for the Bridegroom!

O Lord, who has come, help us wait as those who have a hope. O Lord, who is here, show us how to live as those who are ready. O Lord, who will come again, may we behold your glory at your wedding feast. Amen.

Dr. David Alexander serves as president of Northwest Nazarene University in Nampa, Idaho.

Second Week of Advent

Second Sunday of Advent

STEVE MOORE

MICAH 5:2 · LUKE 2:1–20

And everyone went to their own town to register. So Joseph also went up from the town of Nazareth in Galilee to Judea, to Bethlehem the town of David, because he belonged to the house and line of David. He went there to register with Mary, who was pledged to be married to him and was expecting a child.
LUKE 2:3–5

Places That Matter

Bethlehem. What a small, insignificant place. It wasn't on anyone's radar but the taxman's. Political leaders, religious leaders, business leaders, educational leaders—everyone who was making things happen in the first century, were in the city, or so it seemed (Luke 2:3–4). But who could have guessed that the openness and hospitality of this tiny town would have such profound historical significance? Then, as now, the cities are where the action is! All over the world people continue to move to the city. And yet this little town of Bethlehem enters the Christmas story and becomes the epicenter of an event that will change the world, and reorder history. And it invites us to change the way we look at places, especially the places where we live and work. It is a startling reminder to those of us who live in cities, suburbs, or in the country—place matters. It is not population, commerce, or entertainment that makes the difference about a place. Bethlehem teaches us that openness and hospitality are two of the most important qualities that matter in the economy of God, in places, and in human hearts. Bethlehem had an open manger, and God used it. A small-town girl, Mary, was open to serving God, and Joseph was open to a plan he didn't even fully understand.

History has shown us repeatedly that what often appears to be places (or people) of power or of significance—when taken in a bigger perspective—often lose their sense of importance with the passing of time.

What do you think best describes openness? If you were to define hospitality, what would it consist of? I have often wondered about that innkeeper in Bethlehem. It seems he is often portrayed in Christmas plays as a sort of scrooge, as inhospitable. But I wonder if in fact his opening of the manger was a stretch of his desire to serve a tired, young couple in need, giving hospitality with what he had. Did he later come to realize whom he had hosted? Did he later discover that he had provided a special gift and been a part of something so special? Did he follow the lives of these visitors as their son grew up and made a name for himself? Or was he preoccupied with the cares and pressures of a small business or the worries that plague all of us—not enough time and too much to do? Was his real concern not openness or hospitality, but greed and control?

As we enter the second week of Advent in this journey through the Christmas story, may we slow our lives a bit and open our eyes to see unexpected mercies that may enter our lives quietly but full of promise. May we see the people around us, the places we find ourselves, and the opportunities that present themselves through different eyes. May we exercise the spiritual practices of hospitality and openness such that our place and our lives are open to new and unexpected ways to practice Christmas.

O holy child of Bethlehem!
Descend to us, we pray;
Cast out our sin, and enter in,
Be born in us today![3]

O Lord, who has chosen to dwell in the hearts of those who humble and open themselves, we give thanks that you chose to reveal yourself in an out-of-the-way place. We pray that you would open our eyes and hearts to the miracle of the out-of-the-way place where we find ourselves. Help us to see that your grace and truth are at work all around us, and give us the ears to hear how you may be calling us to join in with you in our place and other places in need of a touch from you. Keep us free of the foolishness of pride, the perceptions of power, or flimsiness of prestige. May we open ourselves this week to the fullness of your grace as we journey through Bethlehem to Christmas joy! Amen.

Steve Moore of the M. J. Murdock Charitable Trust lives in Portland, Oregon, with his wife, Thanne.

Second Monday of Advent

Terry McGonigal

ISAIAH 35:1–10 · LUKE 5:17–26

The desert and the parched land will be glad; the wilderness will rejoice and blossom. Like the crocus, it will burst into bloom; it will rejoice greatly and shout for joy. The glory of Lebanon will be given to it, the splendor of Carmel and Sharon; they will see the glory of the Lord, the splendor of our God.
Isaiah 35:1–2

Some men came carrying a paralyzed man on a mat and tried to take him into the house to lay him before Jesus.
Luke 5:18

When Life Breaks In

As we enter into this second week of Advent, these scripture texts from Isaiah and Luke describe two different ways of viewing reality—how things look from a human viewpoint in contrast with the way God sees our world and our lives. How often we humans look only at the surface and when we don't see anything or anyone that looks interesting or attractive or capable of functioning as a cog in the wheel of our success, we immediately assume there is nothing of worth present. But Isaiah and Luke describe how God looks at a desolate dried-out desert, as well as broken bodies that seem incapable of functioning according to their God-given order. God perceives the possibility of new life and God intervenes to bring that new life into being. Advent is the time at the beginning of the New Year in the church calendar to take off our blinders and try to see as God sees other people and circumstances.

Isaiah 35 describes a familiar scene for the people of Israel, "the wilderness and the dry land." For most of the year most of that part of the Middle East is parched soil, scorched rocks, and vegetation withered by the harsh desert sun. How could any life at all spring forth in that sun-parched wilderness? But, in the spring of each year, the clouds start to build over the Golan Heights, and the moisture gathers in those clouds, and then it starts to rain. The rain comes down and life springs up, for "water will gush forth in the wilderness and streams in the desert" (vs. 6). Then the desert crocus blossoms and the glory of the Lord is seen. Where to our eye no life could happen, it happens.

Luke 5:17–26 records the story of how Jesus, the God-Man, sees what we see—a paralyzed man. But Christ sees more than we are able to see. He looks at the paralyzed man and sees a man made in God's image, and one bound by two disabling sorrows. His sins bind him and his body constrains him. Jesus acts for the healing of the man, breaking the hold of both sorrows (vs. 20, 24). In response, the man leapt to his feet praising God for his restoration, and every witness to the miracle was overwhelmed with amazement, glorifying God (v. 26).

Gracious, loving, and all-seeing God, may this Advent season be a time in which our sight is transformed, so that we can see others as you see them, to hope as you hope, and to be as gracious and merciful as you are to others. May streams flow in the desert places of our lives, and may your abundant life flow through us into the lives of those we encounter as we live in the grace and truth of Jesus. Amen.

Terry McGonigal is the director of Church Engagement at Whitworth University in Spokane, Washington.

Second Tuesday of Advent

FRED DOUGLAS

ISAIAH 40:1–11 · MATTHEW 3:1–2

"In the wilderness prepare the way for the Lord; make straight in the desert a highway for our God."
ISAIAH 40:3

Worth the Wait

As I watched the evening news, I couldn't help noticing how depressed I became before the first commercial break. Darkness and despair, is that what we call news? I thought of my childhood days, when I did not have a care in this world because I was safeguarded by my mom and dad, who intercepted, as much as they could, anything harmful to me.

The people of Israel once had that luxury as well, and then the darkness fell—first the Assyrian invasion, and then the Babylonians, and later the Romans. They suffered mistreatment and were in the bondage of slavery. Being separated from their homeland, they were also discouraged from what felt like abandonment from their God. Oh how they longed to be rescued and delivered from persecution, betrayal (by their own people), and paganism. All they wanted was to be free! Free to worship their God, free to live in harmony with others, and free to be restored to life as God's people in God's place. Where is our God? When is the Messiah coming?

God finally speaks and says (by way of paraphrase), "Prepare the way! Be my messenger; tell everybody that I am keeping my covenant with you. Take delight in my promise, and endure until I come." God wants us to be ready for his arrival.

We have all experienced the pain and challenge of waiting, haven't we? Waiting for a loved one to be healed. Waiting for a child to experience the fruit of hard work. Waiting for a breakthrough in a tough situation. What are you currently waiting for in your life that you need to be reminded to be hopeful?

As John Ortberg wrote, "Biblically, waiting is not just something we have to do until we get what we want. Waiting is part of the process of becoming what God wants us to be."

Christ is coming; get prepared and help prepare others. Don't focus on what hasn't happened; do what is right and uplifting. Then remember what he has promised: "He tends his flock like a shepherd: He gathers the lambs in his arms and carries them close to his heart; he gently leads those that have young" (Isa. 40:11).

In a sense, as preparers, we are the opening band at Jesus' concert. Opening bands don't focus on getting the recognition they deserve. They set the stage for the headliner. Fans are ready to rock precisely because of the opening band.

John the Baptist (see Matthew 3) was Jesus' opening band. He set the stage for Jesus. He did the hard work of playing music for people who had no idea who he was. He challenged people in how they were living their lives. He invited them to live a different way. He didn't monopolize the spotlight—he pointed to Jesus. In doing so, John gave people space to get ready for Jesus' coming.

So, as I watch the evening news, I am reminded that my role is to bring the good news to every situation I encounter. I am to be a voice crying out to those around me—the good news of Jesus, who came into this world to save us from our sin—preparing the way for the Lord!

Father, help me to comfort those around me, showing them your love and your grace. Help me to tenderly speak into the lives of those who are lost and discouraged or have lost hope. Let me be your mouthpiece, an instrument of your love, one that points others to you so that your glory may be revealed for all to clearly see. In Christ's name I pray. Amen.

Fred W. Douglas Jr. serves as the executive director of Portland Youth for Christ and resides in Clackamas, Oregon.

Second Wednesday of Advent

MARY SCHALLER

PSALMS 146:5–10 · MATTHEW 25: 1–13

"The virgin will conceive and give birth to a son, and they will call him Immanuel," (which means "God is with us").
MATTHEW 1:23

We Are Not Alone

When we pray for Christian friends and family, have you ever noticed how often we ask God to be *with* that person in his or her difficulty or challenge? Regardless of whether we're married or single, we all know the value of having someone *with* us as we face each day's trials and celebrate life's joyful moments. It magnifies our joy or reduces the burden when we have someone to share it with us. Having someone *with* us often makes a huge difference in our well-being.

The good news is that we do not have to pray for God to be *with* us. It is already a fact! The historic moment when an angel told a carpenter named Joseph that Mary, the woman he was pledged to marry, was to have a baby, we all gained the opportunity for divine life because of their assent to this mystery. And as Isaiah the prophet had foretold (7:14), so now in Joseph and Mary it came to pass: "The virgin will conceive and give birth to a son, and they will call him Immanuel" (which means "God with us") (Matt. 1:23).

Could it be so simple, that God being *with* us, accompanying us, would be the mechanism of our redemption? Yet this is exactly what God chose to do. It beggars our belief that in our humanness, in our pain, in our sorrows, in our good days, and in our bad ones, God is simply and fully *with* us. All we have to do is to recognize our need for him and to welcome him where God chooses to be—with us!

During Advent each year, it has been valuable to me to be particularly attentive to the fact that Jesus has been *with* me, teaching me, guiding me as I live daily in his Holy Presence. He has reminded me often that everything is possible *with* him. I must confess that even though I've walked *with* Christ for years now, I still forget that he is *there*. I forget also that Christ is there with others, too, and not only with those who know and believe in him. I don't need to be afraid; neither do they. Jesus promised his disciples—and he is trustworthy—that "surely I am with you always, to the very end of the age" (Matt. 28:20).

So when we pray for others and for ourselves, perhaps the prayer that would be best to pray is that we *notice and experience* his presence with us. That's why he came and made a way for us to be reconciled with his Father. That's why his name is Immanuel, or "God with us."

Lord Jesus, I know that you will never leave me nor forsake me; you will answer my soul's deepest longing; that you are all I need. As this world seems to be getting darker, your Word reminds me that you are the light of the world; your life is the light that shines in the darkness and it cannot be extinguished. The victory will be yours. And you will be with anyone who invites you into his or her life. Lord Jesus, may my light shine brightly along with yours in this dark world. Amen.

Mary Schaller is the president of Q Place and currently lives in Sandpoint, Idaho.

Second Thursday of Advent

Walter Wright

EZEKIEL 34:11–16 · JOHN 12:35–36

As a shepherd looks after his scattered flock when he is with them, so will I look after my sheep. I will rescue them from all the places where they were scattered on a day of clouds and darkness.
Ezekiel 34:12

"Believe in the light while you have the light, so that you may become children of the light."
John 12:36

A Light Shines in the Darkness

The other evening we heard the *whump whump whump* of the police helicopter circling our neighborhood. As it hovered overhead, its searchlight probed the bushes and shadows of our neighborhood, seeking out someone hiding there. The relentless light stabbed down into lightless spaces and illuminated them, making hidden things reveal themselves.

Did this intrusion into our neighborhood make us feel safer that night? Perhaps, because we knew that someone was watching over us, looking after us. But it made us notice the darkness close at hand, and what lay hidden there, which intensified our feelings of human vulnerability. The spotlight moving along our street that night was accusing, looking for trouble, and we felt glad that it was not us that the light was seeking. To be forced into a bright circle of light would be uncomfortable, even if we knew that we were not guilty of anything other than living in the neighborhood. Being brought from darkness into the light is threatening to us.

After Ezekiel prophesied against the leaders of Israel for their abuse of leadership, for using their power for their own benefit, and for getting sleek and fat off the flock rather than properly shepherding the people entrusted to them, he proclaimed that God himself will seek out his people and shepherd them well.

As Ezekiel foretold, so God enters our neighborhood to search for his people, to encompass them with love and justice. But unlike the accusatory beam pointing down from a police helicopter, it is the spotlight of God's forgiving love in which we find ourselves caught. Our darkness is illuminated, but we are smothered in God's embrace. The Sovereign Lord God seeks out his people; he searches for us as the protective, generous, and benevolent shepherd who leads with love and justice so that we can thrive as his flock.

In this second week of Advent, we seek to experience more of this probing yet embracing light. As we retell the story of the birth in Bethlehem, spotlighted by the powerful star overhead, we remember that God has in fact searched and found us, entering our neighborhood, embracing our humanity, and placing us in the light of his forgiving love and direction even in a world disfigured by darkness.

But Advent is more than remembering a long-ago time; it is also a present anticipation of and preparation for the coming again of the Shepherd who leads us to the fullness of life in a new creation, when light purifies everything, and where love and justice embrace us forever.

The light from the helicopter that night revealed the darkness around us and made clear to us the vulnerability we felt about bad things hiding in the dark. But this experience caused me to hope for another light, for the ray of the star guiding us to live without fear in the spotlight of God's forgiving love, the light that completely swallows darkness. Maybe this Christmas? Come, Lord Jesus!

Lord, thank you for stepping into the darkness of life and meeting us in the wilderness of our lives. We ask that this season you illuminate the dark spaces in our lives and bring us closer into your joyful light. Today, help us to be honest with our joys and fears, and to bring. Amen.

Walter C. Wright Jr. is a senior fellow at the Max De Pree Center for Leadership in Pasadena, California, where he lives.

Second Friday of Advent

ALAN HOTCHKISS

ISAIAH 61:1–2 · MARK 13:28–37

The Spirit of the Sovereign Lord is on me, because the Lord has anointed me to proclaim good news to the poor. He has sent me to bind up the brokenhearted, to proclaim freedom for the captives and release from darkness for the prisoners, to proclaim the year of the Lord's favor and the day of vengeance of our God, to comfort all who mourn.
ISAIAH 61:1–2

Good News

During his lifetime Jesus became good news for the poor. He comforted the brokenhearted, released captives, freed prisoners, and in so doing, showed each of us how he was genuine good news in the world.

One prisoner in particular was John the Baptist, Jesus' cousin, his greatest advocate and best friend. John had devoted his life to preparing anyone who would listen to him that he for whom Israel had long hoped had appeared. Unfortunately, this message didn't play well with King Herod Antipas, who for other, more personal reasons to do with his marriage, threw John into prison. John was left to wonder whether he had wasted his life, being tempted to doubt whether Jesus was the Messiah for whom Israel had hoped.

For John to know *that* Jesus was the One was not the same thing as John knowing *how* Jesus would act as the Messiah. And so John, "calling two of [his disciples], he sent them to the Lord to ask, 'Are you the one who is to come, or should we expect someone else?'" (Luke 7:18–19). Jesus' answer is revealing. "Go back and report to John what you have seen and heard: The blind receive sight, the lame walk, those who have leprosy are cleansed, the deaf hear, the dead are raised, and the good news is proclaimed to the poor. Blessed is anyone who does not stumble on account of me" (Luke 7:22–23). In this response to his best friend, Jesus went to the heart of how he intended to be Messiah, and described to John what taking the good news to the poor really means.

Jesus committed his life and his power to reverse cases of personal injustice that humans were compelled to accept by forces out of their control. Which one of us decides to be blind, or crippled? Who prays for their child to be deaf? Who looks for an opportunity to become a leper? Is anyone excited about dying?

Jesus was reminding his dear friend that *he is the One* who has the power to reverse every injustice. *Jesus is good news* for the poor, or anyone who has suffered injustice.

If Jesus were on Earth today, he might put it like this: "Were you crippled physically or emotionally? Has an oppressive system or boss held you back? Were you born not in the rich world, but in the rest of the world? Have you lost someone to death? Will you eventually face it yourself? Are you ineligible for a relationship with your Creator because Adam and Eve embedded evil into your nature as a human? I have stood in the gap for you." We are all poor, and Jesus' defeat of all injustice is our *good news*.

Let us celebrate the birth of this human baby who became good news to all of us who are poor. And may we also embody his good news, fighting every injustice we see with his mercy and grace in the days ahead.

O God our Father and our Lord Jesus Christ, we are all poor; we have been wounded by life; we are in need of your good news. Lord Jesus, come freshly into our hearts this season. Open our eyes to your power activated against earthly injustice, both in our own lives and in the lives of those who are within our reach. Jesus, thank you for coming humbly to the earth. For sneaking up on us, even as your prophets prepared, loudly, for your arrival. Lord Jesus we come to you in our poverty, looking to you as our very own good news. You are our only hope. Amen.

Alan Hotchkiss is the US executive director of Africa New Life Ministries and lives in Portland, Oregon.

Second Saturday of Advent

Yolanda Spiva

JEREMIAH 29:11 · PSALM 136:1

"For I know the plans I have for you," declares the Lord,
"plans to prosper you and not to harm you,
plans to give you hope and a future."
Jeremiah 29:11

Give thanks to the Lord, for he is good. His love endures forever.
Psalm 136:1

There Is Hope

When the prophet Jeremiah declared to the people of Israel (whom Nebuchadnezzar had exiled to Babylon) that their unwanted and forced relocation to a place of turmoil, war, and instability was actually a part of God's plan for them, their discomfort about, and disbelief of, this message was strongly felt. Despite their considerable resistance to accepting this, history did prove that God was faithful to his people in their exile, and that he blessed them there.

Though we may not always understand, agree with, or appreciate the places or circumstances into which the Lord puts us (guided by the Holy Spirit), we do begin to understand how poorly we see what God is doing. We may perceive a circumstance to be a forced exile, a removal from a place of comfort into a place of discomfort (whether literally or figuratively, spiritually or physically), yet later we grasp it to be part of God's master plan for our lives. His master plan ultimately eludes us, but we learn to trust that he does lead us through our challenges into times of enduring peace, prosperity, and hope for the future.

When we find ourselves in these situations of exile, we question the Lord about our difficult circumstances. Yet we learn that God appreciates our inquiries, and we come to see how our questions keep us in direct relationship with him, and that they deepen a loving, intimate, nurturing union with him. Our ability to grow stronger and not weaker through experiences of exile increases in direct proportion to our commitment to be taught by God's Holy Word and in fellowship with other Christian believers on a similar path.

When we realize that we have become resentful, or lament where God has placed us in fulfillment of his divine purposes in and through us, we must shed these unproductive feelings of anger, disappointment, or regret, and replace them with expressions of thanksgiving to the Lord, for he is indeed good. Giving thanks to the Lord while operating in obedience to his purpose and plans for our lives, allows us to experience the enduring nature of his love, mercy, and faithfulness.

Lord, thank you for your love. Thank you for your manifold expressions of love—to, through, for, and from us. Lord, because of your love and your goodness, we trust you. We trust that every decision and destination to which you have guided us has been for our good and not for our destruction. Therefore, we will not give in to feelings of anger or regret. Lord, help us to appreciate the brand-new mercies you dispense upon us daily, and teach us to expect from you a future full of hope and prosperity. Father, for these, and for all our blessings, we thank you, in the mighty and matchless name of your son, Jesus. Amen.

Yolanda Watson Spiva PhD is the president and CEO of the College Success Foundation in Washington State.

Third Week of Advent

Third Sunday of Advent

FR. RICK GANZ

ISAIAH 60:1–3 · MATTHEW 17:9–13

The disciples asked him, "Why then do the teachers of the law say that Elijah must come first?"
MATTHEW 17:10

The One Who Comes First

The disciples asked a question of Jesus that he did not answer. Instead of answering *why*, Jesus answered *that* Elijah had come. John the Baptist was like Elijah and was present in the midst. Yet their question remained an interesting one: *Why* do the scribes teach that . . . ? Well, they found it taught in Malachi 4:5: "See, I will send the prophet Elijah to you before that great and dreadful day of the Lord comes." But this fact still leaves unexplored why there needed to be a herald or forerunner in the first place.

As we become more familiar with the Scriptures, we gain familiarity with how God tends to think and act, and therefore where God is *likely* to show up in a particular set of circumstances, and how God is likely to proceed there. Much of the art of discernment lies in gaining such familiarity with God, who he is, and how we may know him.

It is my conviction that often God does not answer our prayers in the way that we think he will, or should. Consider the following: we ask God that a particular grace be given us. And whether we notice it or not, we tend in such moments to look upward in the privacy of our own imagination, looking up toward God as we intercede for the grace, wanting the grace to come down. (The geometry of our prayer life is most interesting to ponder.)

Even though what we usually ask of God must come to us sideways, if you will, from another human being (a job; an opportunity; forgiveness; friendship; and so forth), we look up and ask that God give it to us. And without noticing what we do, we overlook the person right next to us whom God has sent us to give it—"'Men of Galilee,' they said, 'why do you stand here looking into the sky?'" (Acts 1:11). We are not familiar with how God delights to work.

Over the course of our lives, we ask God to give us much and more. But I have learned that God's *typical* response is to *send us to each other*. Through friendship with each other we will often be given what and more than what we need. Through friendship we often discover that the things we thought essential, are not. And things we have overlooked—become essential and important to our lives!

Here, then, is the real grace for us to ponder during Advent. It is to *recognize* who God sends to us, noticing when he does, and to open in friendship toward him or her. We need to learn how to look up, if you will, when we pray, but also to look sideways for those whom God sends to us. In God's typical way, every friend becomes God's herald and forerunner.

So, back to Elijah as herald and forerunner, and why he is that? The people prayed for the Messiah to come. In typical fashion, God in the fullness of time gave them John instead (not the Messiah), a herald and forerunner, but through whom, and by his example and teaching, they would be given the answer to their prayer when suddenly he appeared—"The next day John saw Jesus coming toward him and said, 'Look, the Lamb of God, who takes away the sin of the world!'" (John 1:29).

Advent is a season, but also a practice, that helps us prepare and open our lives for the coming of Christ in our world and to those around us who help us receive his grace and love. Gracious Lord, give us the grace to recognize the people you send to us, asking less for particular graces and more for good people to be sent to us to welcome as your heralds and forerunners . . . and our friends. May we become heralds of the Lamb of God in our world and with our friends. Amen.

Fr. Rick Ganz, SJ has been a Jesuit and Roman Catholic priest for forty years, and is a teacher, writer, and spiritual director residing in Portland, Oregon.

Third Monday of Advent

Christine Sine

PSALMS 98 · 2 CORINTHIANS 4:6

"For God, who said, 'Let light shine out of darkness,' made his light shine in our hearts to give us the light of the knowledge of God's glory displayed in the face of Christ."
2 *Corinthians* 4:6

Overcoming Darkness

I once flew from New Zealand to Norway at the beginning of December, from the light of long summer evenings to the dark of midwinter. Suddenly in Norway the night crashed in on me early in the afternoon, and I struggled to adjust. Then I became aware of the Christmas lights. They festooned the trees and lit up candelabras in the windows. They hung like icicles from the eaves and glowed through ice sculptures in front of houses. Most breathtaking of all, they shone in stars that hung over rooftops and crowned the light-enshrouded trees.

Growing up in the southern hemisphere, where Christmas falls in the middle of summer, Christmas lights held little meaning for me except as pretty decorations. Until that visit to Norway, I had never really appreciated the impact of light in a darkened world. But to my light-starved eyes, those Christmas lights were lifesaving, and my soul feasted on their brilliant display.

In Jesus' day, light shining in the darkness promised safety and protection. A candle or fire on a dark night literally saved lives. The monsters that lurked in the darkness were not imaginary. Lions, bears, and predators of all kinds could be drawn to the vulnerable humans who lacked the protection and safety of the light of a fire: terror and fear must have gripped people's hearts when their fire went out and there was no dry tinder with which to start a new one. Today, even when we are miles from the city, the horizon glows with myriad dots from distant streetlights. Imagine what travelers two thousand years ago would have given for an electric light that could not be snuffed out by a gust of wind or a deluge of rain.

For the people who read Paul's words, the imagery of light in the darkness was a reality in the experience of life in the midst of danger and death. The promise of Christ's coming into their hearts brought with it the assurance of safety and security in the midst of the terrors of the world in which they lived.

I long to see Christ's light shine as brilliantly in our world today as these words promise. I am sometimes overwhelmed by the darkness brought by the loss of thousands of young children and innocents that die every day from hunger, war, and disease. While light is much more a part of our world than in the biblical world, the need for safety, hope, and security is even greater. The Christmas season reminds us and challenges us to become the ones who spread and shine the lights of Christ into every dark corner of the world. We should be reassured by the promise and the hope that it brings. Where his light is, there is Christ too.

Lord God Almighty, may the light of Christ
truly shine in us, through us, and around us.
May it fill our hearts and flow out into our
dark and troubled world. Amen.

Christine Sine is executive director of Mustard Seed Associates, currently living in Seattle, Washington.

Third Tuesday of Advent

Rita Nussli

ISAIAH 61:1–4 · LUKE 1:26–38

"I am the Lord's servant," Mary answered.
"May your word to me be fulfilled."
Luke 1:38

Deep into the Word

I invite you to read Luke 1:26–38, using the ancient practice of *lectio divina* (Latin for "divine reading"). In this practice, we are encouraged to read the Word of God slowly, like a love letter, asking the Holy Spirit to be our teacher as we read the passage four times, savoring every word, quietly reflecting on thoughts the Holy Spirit brings. In our first reading (*lectio*), we pay careful attention to the words. Which words shimmer and draw our attention? As we thoughtfully read the passage a second time, we use our active imagination, placing ourselves in the story (*meditatio*). This engages us at the level of the heart, where memory, experience, thoughts, feelings, hopes, desires, and intentions are joined. This is where we are likely to discover what a given passage means for us personally. In our third reading, we seek to form a spoken prayer that flows naturally from our meditation (*oratio*). This prayer is our first response to what we have assimilated in the first two phases of spiritual reading. With the fourth reading and throughout the day, we practice contemplation (*comtemplatio*) of what we experienced. No expectations, no demands—just the desire to be in the divine presence, receptive to whatever God wills to do with and for us through contemplating or thinking about the scripture all day long.

As we think about Luke 1:26–38, the idea of "highly favored" prompts us to wonder along with Mary, are we truly favored by our God?—"You will conceive and give birth to a son, and you are to call him Jesus. He will be great and will be called the Son of the Most High. The Lord God will give him the throne of his father David, and he will reign over Jacob's descendants forever; his kingdom will never end" (Luke 1:31–33). These words leap off the page and bring a sense of awe to our hearts. Mary is being asked to give birth to the Messiah, and in turn we find ourselves asking if we are being invited to birth something in partnership with God. Mary asked a simple question, "How will this be, since I am a virgin?" Gabriel's response shakes us: "The Holy Spirit will come on you, and the power of the Most High will overshadow you" (vv. 34–35). What would it feel like to have the power of the Most High overshadow us? What could we create? Next we read of Elizabeth: "Even Elizabeth your relative is going to have a child in her old age, and she who was said to be unable to conceive is in her sixth month. For no word from God will ever fail" (vv. 36–37). Really? Nothing is impossible with God? Do we believe this? Perhaps in our heads. What would we do, how would we live, if these words became an experiential truth woven into the very fabric of our being: "May it be to me as you have said." Does Mary realize what she is saying yes to? Will Joseph, her soon-to-be husband, stay with her? Who will believe she is a virgin giving birth to the Son of God? Will she be stoned by the righteous for this seeming sin of sexual promiscuity? As these words sink into our inner thoughts we ask: Am I willing to risk everything to partner with God in every aspect of the activities of my life? Will I say, as Mary did, "I am the Lord's servant. . . . May your word to me be fulfilled" (Luke 1:38)?

Lord God, I would be silent now and expectant, ready to be taught by your Holy Spirit through your Word. May I receive the gift I need, so I may become the gift others need. Amen.

Rita Nussli is the associate director of Soul Formation and lives in Seattle, Washington.

Third Wednesday of Advent

Keith Anderson

PSALM 146 · REVELATION 1:1–8

He is the Maker of heaven and earth, the sea, and everything in them—he remains faithful forever. He upholds the cause of the oppressed and gives food to the hungry. The Lord sets prisoners free, the Lord gives sight to the blind, the Lord lifts up those who are bowed down, the Lord loves the righteous. The Lord watches over the foreigner and sustains the fatherless and the widow, but he frustrates the ways of the wicked.
Psalm 146:6–9

You Are Neighbor

God loves justice, and sets a table for food, freedom, sight, and care. The troubling and encouraging truth is that God moved into the neighborhood where we live. He cares.

The surprise of Advent is not *that* Messiah comes, but *where* he comes, and *what* he comes to do. "'I am the Alpha and the Omega,' says the Lord God, 'who is, and who was, and who is to come, the Almighty'" (Rev. 1:8). As a child I would picture that coming one as from above and massive, grand, and fearsome—almighty and vast.

The writer of the psalm had a different picture of the one for whom we wait in Advent. He pictured Yahweh as the host at a neighborhood food bank and community center. In stark contrast to the powerful politicians and rulers (princes), God sets the table to give food to the hungry, to execute justice for those oppressed, to watch over strangers, widows, and orphans—vulnerable ones who need a system that offers a new way in a context of deathliness and oppression. The new way is the dramatic picture that forms for us in Advent: Jesus moved into the neighborhood.

I was born in a neighborhood on the far south side of Chicago. It was a melting pot of European Americans who moved into tiny bungalows on Sangamon Street—Swedish, Irish, Scottish, English, Polish, and Italian. Many of us were the children of first-generation Americans. The story of my earliest years was the story of neighborhood. Seventy-Ninth Street for church. Fifty-Ninth Street for furniture. Ninety-Fifth and Halstead for groceries. Mount Vernon for grammar school. We played ball in the street until the next car came along. We played in the field vacated by the steel mill located nearby. Johnson, Petkus, Galoonagus, Maher, McCabe, and Anderson were my neighbors, just to name a few.

Advent is also the story of neighborhood, but it comes with a problem: Jesus in the crèche is not the problem. Angels and magi are not the trouble. What God is doing in the neighborhood is the problem. God brings justice, and sets a table for food, freedom, sight, and care. The troubling truth is that God moved into the neighborhood where we live.

It troubles us because it moves us from superficial seeing to sacramental seeing: if we have eyes to see this great mystery, we see deep into everyday reality; there is something more going on. That's where the trouble starts. If Jesus moved into the neighborhood, we must ask: "Will I follow him where he goes, learn what he does, and join him?" If Jesus inhabits the flesh, he lives in flesh; if Jesus inhabits time and space, he lives where we live—in the neighborhood of our lives. And that changes everything. Advent is a startling declaration to an audacious invitation: if you believe what these scriptures say, you are invited to see God in your homes, schools, businesses, hospitals, community centers, banks, and churches. God walking the streets as you make decisions about all of the places where you have influence: spiritual, financial, social, human, and intellectual. God is interested in the most human parts of your life: family and work, recreation and thinking, and everything else we do.

The amazing, troubling, and hopeful truth is that God moved into the neighborhood where we live, and that changes everything. This Christmas season may we join him in new ways in the creative ways he is at work in our world.

I pray for eyes to see the living God walking in my neighborhood in this season of Advent. Give me the eyes to see the neighborhood and world the way you do. Give me the courage to join you where you are at work. Amen.

Dr. Keith R. Anderson is the president of the Seattle School of Theology and Psychology and lives in Seattle, Washington.

Third Thursday of Advent

Randy Roberts

PSALMS 80:1–7 · PHILIPPIANS 4:4–9

Do not be anxious about anything, but in every situation, by prayer and petition, with thanksgiving, present your requests to God. And the peace of God, which transcends all understanding, will guard your hearts and your minds in Christ Jesus.
Philippians 4:6–7

The Genuine Pathway to a God-Given Peace

While memorizing scripture is a wise practice, using flash cards with a verse or two written on them can be perilous. Why? Because when verses are extracted from their biblical context, we may, or are likely, to misinterpret them. This will, predictably, lead to misunderstanding and misapplying the text. Consider the following example.

Embedded in Philippians 4:4–9 are the consoling words of verses 6 and 7 that are often memorized and claimed as a promise. While they do indeed contain an antidote to *inappropriate* anxiety (the same word is used for legitimate concern in Philippians 2:20 and 2 Corinthians 11:28), what these verses actually reveal concerning a remedy for anxiety is only partially understood outside of its broader context.

In Philippians 4, Paul gave a series of exhortations about what it means to "stand firm in the Lord" (v. 1). In verses 2–3 he exhorted Euodia and Syntyche to be reconciled with each other, and then to rejoice in the Lord (v. 4), and to manifest a gentle/considerate/yielding spirit when interacting with others (v. 5a), remembering the Lord's nearness (referring both to his omnipresence and to his imminent return) as an incentive to obey and to accept as a source of comfort in times of trouble (v. 5b).

In vv. 6–7, Paul promised that those who fight the anxiety they feel, entrusting their concerns to God in grateful prayer, will experience the transcendent, heart-guarding peace of God.

Because "finally" introduces verse 8, we assume that Paul is now changing topics. But when we read verse 9, we see that it concludes with a promise that "the God of *peace*" will be with those whose lives reflect the same kind of obedience found in Paul himself. Surely experiencing the "peace of God" and the "God of peace" are somehow related.

If verses 6–7 explain how to experience the peace of God, and verse 9 speaks of how to experience the God of peace, verse 8 explains what kind of person we each must become to experience both. So Paul's prescription for peace is not just a one-point sermon ("to experience peace, pray"). Instead he added at least two more points: we must also maintain a pure and edifying thought life (v. 8), and our lives must reflect appropriate obedience (v. 9).

This makes good sense. Should we expect God's peace to dwell in us if our thoughts dwell on that which is unedifying and contaminating? Similarly, how can such peace exist when we are living in deliberate disobedience to the God who grants it?

Christ came to enable those who, through faith in him, have peace *with* God to also experience the peace *of* God. But we will only do so if we follow fully his wise prescription for that blessing.

Our Father, in light of the many challenges that accompany lives lived out in a fallen world, we are so grateful for the peace that you grant those who trust in you, and who live out that trust by seeking to obey you in both attitude and action. Please deepen both our faith and our devotion so that we may experience more fully, and model more compellingly, the kind of life that you desire for us. Amen.

Randal Roberts is president and professor of spiritual formation at Western Seminary in Portland, Oregon.

Third Friday of Advent

Bob Lonac

JOHN 15: 4–5

"Remain in me, as I also remain in you. No branch can bear fruit by itself; it must remain in the vine. Neither can you bear fruit unless you remain in me. I am the vine; you are the branches. If you remain in me and I in you, you will bear much fruit; apart from me you can do nothing."
John 15:4–5

He Is Here!

As we celebrate Jesus' birth and study his life, we find that Jesus' claims in John 15:4–5 are astonishing! The parable of the vine and the branches, and the specific verses in this scripture, are one stark example of the unusual claims Christ made. "Apart from me you can do nothing."

Really? I do things every day apart from you, don't I?

"If you remain in me, and I in you, you will bear much fruit." What this fruit of remaining in him looks like is defined clearly in Galatians 5:22–23: "But the fruit of the Spirit is love, joy, peace, forbearance, kindness, goodness, faithfulness, gentleness and self-control. Against such things there is no law."

Nothing can hold back the impact of people who exemplify these traits. The claim of Christ is that he, through his Holy Spirit, will abide in us and bring fruitfulness that works its way through us from the inside out. The fruit of the Spirit listed in

Galatians, when lived out in our everyday lives, has an impact on those around us that can be deep and profound. They bring the aroma of Christ himself into our lives and our relationships. They are at the core of God's transforming power. And they comprise the exact strategy he has to transform our world.

Jesus is alive and active today through the work of the Holy Spirit in our lives. The coming of Christ into the world opened up unfathomable opportunities for us to reflect his glory to a world that is incredibly needy and ready for the good news that *he is here*! And as we open up our hearts to the work of his Spirit, our lives abiding in Christ will make sense to us and bring joy to those around us.

Lord Jesus, this season we open our hearts
and minds to the work of your Spirit in our
lives. Thank you for your unconditional
love that passes all understanding.
Lord, flood our hearts with this love so that we may
love one another. Make us fruitful in our lives so
that others may experience your love and peace this
Christmas season and beyond. Thank you for coming
into the world to make this all possible. Amen.

Bob Lonac is the president and CEO of CRISTA Ministries and lives in Edmonds, Washington.

Third Saturday of Advent

Andrea Cook

PSALMS 89:1–4 · LUKE 3:1–6

In the fifteenth year of the reign of Tiberius Caesar—when Pontius Pilate was governor of Judea, Herod tetrarch of Galilee, his brother Philip tetrarch of Iturea and Traconitis, and Lysanias tetrarch of Abilene—during the high-priesthood of Annas and Caiaphas, the word of God came to John son of Zechariah in the wilderness.
Luke 3:1–2

Politics Aside, God Is on the Move

Throughout my nearly thirty-eight-year career in higher education—five different institutions—I have worked each day with the bright minds and earnest followers of Jesus. When I reflect on the assignments that I have accepted, and on the reasons I have changed roles or institutions, I recognize how God has been on the move in my life. I know he has been making a way in the world, using my surrendered life to provide unique and special opportunities for me to serve him and the world.

However, if I am honest, there have been moments along the way when the political realities through which I have navigated, and the points of pressure that led to a change have not always felt to me like a blessing or a spiritual experience.

Now, in hindsight, I can perceive how my tested faith, and my willingness to trust God, have put me in a position to acknowledge that my experience and my expertise have converged nearly perfectly. I am grateful for the challenges of my life, clearly seeing how my current assignment is a fulfillment of what God has done for me, and because of me, and who God has called me to become.

Luke 3:1–6 shows that God's great rescue plan—Jesus of Nazareth—disrupted the political realities of first-century Israel, as well as disrupting the lives and purposes of those seeking control throughout all times and places. John the Baptist's prophetic role began in the "fifteenth year of the reign of Tiberius Caesar," when Rome controlled Palestine, and when, in spite of peace the region was experiencing, the differences between Rome and Israel habitually spawned significant political tensions.

For Luke, John was the foremost prophetic messenger of God, who warned of accountability to God, and who announced the approach of God's salvation. Those with power and political position throughout world history have questioned whether or not the salvation of God, through Jesus Christ, is in fact able to make the crooked ways straight or the rough ways smooth.

No matter how complicated the politics we face, Luke 3 reminds us that God is on the move. Our human tendency is to strategize or manipulate our circumstances. We want more power; not less. We seek positions that are safe as we search for the high ground.

Advent is sometimes defined as the "arrival of a notable person, thing, or event." When I could not in my own life see clearly into the future, I put my full weight on the idea that John the Baptist's prophetic message must be true. God has a way through this world and its complexities. His way is better than mine. And so we take courage that as we live into the promise of the kingdom of God, our future rests comfortably in the hands of a King who loves us and pursues us just as creatively now as he did more than two thousand years ago.

Lord, you know our path and you see much farther ahead than we do. Please give us faith to trust that you are on the move in our lives and in the world around us. Amen.

Dr. Andrea Cook is the president of Warner Pacific College in Portland, Oregon, where she lives.

Fourth Week of Advent

Fourth Sunday of Advent

STEVE MOORE

DANIEL 7:13–14 · LUKE 2:8–20

The shepherds said to one another "Let's go to Bethlehem and see this thing that has happened, which the Lord has told us about."
LUKE 2:15

Live Like a Shepherd

What profession does God use the most for his purposes? Perhaps when we first hear such a question, our thoughts turn to ministers or missionaries, evangelists or Bible teachers—people in special religious roles. But after a few moments of reflection, we know that isn't true. We remember that no job or profession guarantees that the person filling it is about God's purposes or even receptive to God's leading. Just as we have learned in recent weeks in our reflections that there is no certain place or time that guarantees God's presence, there is no special profession that guarantees God's purposes being done in the world or hearing God's voice. Enter the shepherds and the angels!

We are again reminded by the shepherds that God's chief criterion for being a person of his purposes is openness. Shepherds were probably among the lowest of professions in the first century. But in an amazing and surprising act of grace, God chose the shepherds as those who would be given the startling news that God had come to live among us, and he was starting out the same way we all do—as a baby!

However, one cannot read the complete passage in Luke and say the shepherds were immediately open and receptive. Scripture makes it clear they were scared spitless! And rightly so: there was light, there was music, there were angels—and a shocking message, a king was born, nearby! But while the angels made sure to get the shepherds' attention, I believe it took a while for all that was said that night to sink in. I sometimes fear in our modern world that we live our lives trying to control things so much and, at the same time, are so distracted by all the world's Tinkertoys that we often miss God breaking into our world.

In our media-saturated, sensory-overloaded world, we are tempted to say to ourselves, "I've seen it all; nothing can shock me anymore." In his *Letters to Malcolm*, C. S. Lewis reflected, "We shall not be able to adore God on the highest occasions if we have not learned a habit of doing so in the lowest. At best, our faith and reason will tell us that He is adorable, but if we have not personally found Him to be adorable, than we have not known him, not tasted and seen."[4]

Maybe part of our commitment this Christmas season needs to be an openness to make ourselves available to the astonishment and wonder of God taking on flesh in the person of Jesus and coming into *our* world! May we cultivate in ourselves what is often sung, "O come, let us adore him." May we practice adoration.

Lord, we pray that you would cultivate wonder in us. Give us the hearts of the shepherds who embraced that which they couldn't fully understand and risked following even when everything wasn't completely clear. As we journey these final days to Christmas Day, may we travel with an expectancy, no matter what is going on in our world, that we will set our course by the one who made the stars. Amen.

Steve Moore of the M. J. Murdock Charitable Trust lives in Portland, Oregon, with his wife, Thanne.

Fourth Monday of Advent

JUDY KLAUSTERMEYER

ISAIAH 40:28–29 · LUKE 1:39–45

"Blessed is she who has believed that the Lord would fulfill his promises to her!"
LUKE 1:45

Stepping Forward in Faith

The angel Gabriel, one of God's chief messengers, stood before the young, small-town virgin and spoke to her by name. His message was literally unbelievable, that she would be the mother of the long-awaited Messiah! It was unbelievable on at least three counts: that she had been chosen; that the Messiah would come at last; and that she would remain a virgin, bearing a child conceived by the Holy Spirit. Mary was stunned almost speechless, but the angel offered her the support of her childless, elderly relative Elizabeth, wife of a priest, who was also having a miracle baby. No wonder Mary rushed to Elizabeth's side! Who better to help her through that frightening time?

Mary's response to the angel was simple and humble: she believed and accepted. In a moment that was all mystery, utterly beyond her understanding, Mary chose to trust God with her life, and the Savior of all creation was conceived in her.

Don't you wonder about Mary's thoughts during that journey from Nazareth in the north to the hill country of Judea in the south? Was she attacked by doubt? Did she imagine all the agonizing possibilities of Joseph's reactions to her news? Was she filled with fear and hope and joy at the thought of being mother to the Messiah? Did she rehearse every imaginable response of her family members?

And yet in the midst of it all, there was in her a core of knowing and obedience, a place where she said, "Lord, I put my faith and trust in you." As Saint Paul later wrote, "Yet this is no cause for shame, because I know *whom* I have believed, and am convinced that he is able to guard what I have entrusted to him until that day" (2 Tim. 1:12, italics added).

The moment that Mary walked through Elizabeth's door, we imagine her doubts and fears are magnificently allayed. In shock and amazement, before she said more than Elizabeth's name, she heard Elizabeth loudly proclaim her as "the mother of my Lord"! Even the unborn baby John in Elizabeth's womb leapt for joy! And then Elizabeth spoke the words that ring through all eternity: "Blessed is she who has *believed* that what the Lord has said to her will be accomplished."

Mary's *belief* pivoted history away from that fatal moment in the original Paradise when Eve was tempted with "Did God really say . . . ?" Now here was from Mary an unconditional "yes" to what God did really say to her through the angel Gabriel. And because of this, "to us a child is born, to us a son is given" (Isa. 9:6).

This child of the Holy Spirit, born of Mary's belief, is also *our* child. We have been given a son. For as surely as Mary conceived because she believed what God said, so also does God give birth to himself spiritually in our souls when we hear the gospel message and really believe it. The mystery and wonder and accomplishment of God's Word remain to this day. Blessed is the one who believes.

Father, Son, and Holy Spirit, we believe. Help our unbelief. We gladly embrace your birth in our souls. May your Word be accomplished in us. To the glory and honor of Jesus, Amen.

Judy Klaustermeyer serves as one of the directors of Young Life's Women's Leadership Network and lives in Mesa, Washington.

Fourth Tuesday of Advent

DONALD MANNING

MICAH 5:2–5 · LUKE 1:5–25

"How will this be," Mary asked the angel, "since I am a virgin?"
LUKE 1:34

Living in Awe

In the first chapter of Luke's gospel, the angel Gabriel was quite busy, appearing first to Zechariah to foretell the birth of John the Baptist, and then to Mary to foretell the birth of Jesus. The parallels between Zechariah and Mary offer insight not only in the way we prepare for the birth of Christ, but how in our day-to-day lives we should stand humbled and in awe of God. Standing in awe of God is a good reminder of a posture we should assume more often than not!

When Gabriel appeared to Zechariah, he was terrified. Why? He was, after all, a righteous man living blamelessly according to all God's commandments, praying in the temple. Of all people in all places, why was he terrified? Even more curious, when Gabriel told Zechariah that God had answered his lifelong prayer, and Elizabeth, his wife, would give birth to the great John the Baptist, this righteous and blameless priest became suddenly confused and doubtful. He asked, "How can I be sure of this?" (v. 18). His question was laced with a sense of entitlement, doubt, and fear.

Compare Mary's response to the sudden appearance of Gabriel. She was perplexed by his greeting, not terrified. She couldn't fathom why Gabriel called her "favored one of God." She was not an elder, a priest, or a man of rank. She was one step above chattel, a young virgin betrothed to an older man. Even more startling, Gabriel told her that she would give birth to Jesus, the Son of the Most High. Unlike Zechariah, Mary did not ask for proof. Rather, she was awestruck, "How will this be, since I am a virgin?" (v. 34).

Many men and women in the developing parts of the world often live on less than $1.50 a day. When they rise with the sun, the single question they ask is: How will I feed my family today? Yet, they offer their lives; indeed, they offer this very question of life and death to God. They rest in God's mercy.

Returning from any developing country is often jarring and unnerving. I become Zechariah, a decent man trying to live blamelessly, but falling into the trap of entitlement, doubt, and fear. I wake from a soft bed to a warm shower and I ask: What will I wear today; why am I out of toothpaste; and what am I going to make for dinner? Like Zechariah, my subconscious sense of entitlement often leads to callousness, doubt, and needless anxiety.

The poor, the lowly, the least among us so often mirror the unimaginable humility of God, who became flesh and blood simply to be closer to us. Too often our over-amped, market-driven culture leaches humility out of us and replaces it with entitlement, fear, and doubt. This Advent, as you wait for the birth of Jesus and all that his coming into the world implies, try starting your morning with a quiet moment of awe and wonder; try asking, like Mary: How will this be?

Loving God, I stand before you this morning holding all that I am, all my thoughts, and all my questions, in sacred silence. I offer this to you because it is all that I have to offer. I pray that you would take these thoughts and these questions, that you would take my whole life and transform it into an eternal prayer of awe and wonder at your unending and unconditional love. Today, in this moment, I start fresh in your love. Today, in this stillness with you, I let go of my pride, of my need to know, and I breathe in your comfort and peace. Amen.

Don Manning is the president and CEO of Agros International in Seattle, Washington, where he lives.

Fourth Wednesday of Advent

CARY PAINE

ISAIAH 45:2–8 · LUKE 21:25–36

"For the sake of Jacob my servant, of Israel my chosen, I summon you by name and bestow on you a title of honor, though you do not acknowledge me. I am the Lord, and there is no other; apart from me there is no God. I will strengthen you, though you have not acknowledged me, so that from the rising of the sun to the place of its setting people may know there is none besides me. I am the Lord, and there is no other."
ISAIAH 45:4–6

No Ordinary Night

In times of crisis, we all want a faith that can stand up and sustain us. A faith that helps us weather the inevitable storms and challenges of life.

But just as important, we need a faith that works in the ordinary times, day in and day out, when life is routine—when we are trying to achieve some sense of balance as we juggle expectations and responsibilities in our work, with family and friends, and in matters of personal well-being. What does our faith in ordinary times have to say to us then?

How do we handle the ordinary in our current culture? What do we think about when we stand in line at the grocery store, or ride in an elevator, or when we sit in traffic? We are constantly bombarded by information sound bites—and yet, paradoxically, I'm not sure we think about much at all. Mobile technology has changed our behavior. Seldom are we ever alone with our thoughts these days. Instead, we're talking or texting, tweeting or posting. Look around you on the bus, or on a crowded city street. Is anyone alone with his or her thoughts? It doesn't seem so, perhaps because the alternative of social media is too enticing, or because we're simply uncomfortable with introspection. Too often, we just don't want to go inside ourselves. "Silence is frightening," wrote Dallas Willard, "because it strips us as nothing else does, throwing us upon the stark realities of our life."[5] Perhaps Pascal was right when he wrote, "All men's miseries derive from not being able to sit in a quiet room alone." We all experience alone time, but instead of taking advantage of the possibilities, we get entangled in busyness or we do whatever we can to avoid the solitude. But if this is what is ordinary for us, then how possibly can an everyday faith take hold of us and deepen?

Reflection, meditation, and voluntary inactivity have all become lost disciplines. If we were to "sit in a quiet room alone," perhaps we could be more attentive to our relationship with God, speaking and listening to him. But where would we start if we were alone with our thoughts? Let me suggest that the Lord's words in Isaiah 45 might provide a good beginning. In eight verses, the Lord provides these remarkable reassurances. "I will go before you. . . . [I will] cut through bars of iron. . . . [I will give you] riches stored in secret places. . . . I summon you by name and bestow on you a title of honor. . . . I will strengthen you. . . . I form the light. . . . I bring prosperity. . . . I, the Lord, do all these things." Wherever our thoughts might take us in the ordinary moments of life, could recalling these reassuring words help make our faith more meaningful and resourceful?

It was an ordinary night in Bethlehem when God broke through in the form of a baby, changing permanently the meaning of ordinary. It was the time of a census, and everybody was busy in the routines of life. Who paid any attention to a woman in labor as she gave birth to a son in a barn? I wonder if Mary recalled the words of the angel Gabriel in those waiting moments. Did she understand that the infant in her arms, so vulnerable and weak in appearance, was the same divineness who made such remarkable promises through the prophet Isaiah centuries before? God speaks to us loudly in ordinary moments. Can we be more attentive? Dare we be still, and know that he is God? We would do well to learn how to listen to his Spirit and his voice.

Father, God of the extraordinary and the ordinary,
remind us that we are never alone with our thoughts.
You are always present, to strengthen and to
guide us. Continue to speak to us, and help
us to be attentive to what you are saying.
In Jesus' name, amen.

Cary Paine is the president of the Stewardship Foundation in Tacoma, Washington.

Fourth Thursday of Advent

PATRICE TSAGUE

MATTHEW 4:16 · PSALM 36:9

"The people living in darkness have seen a great light; on those living in the land of the shadow of death a light has dawned."
MATTHEW 4:16

"For with you is the fountain of life; in your light we see light."
PSALM 36:9

The Light of the World

As we prepare our hearts and minds for the greatest time of the year, we are reminded of God's mercy and his sacrificial gift to the world. During this time, however, we cannot help but be saddened at times by the reality of our own limitations. Despite all the innovations, human creativity, and discoveries that humankind has uncovered, there are children around the world who still die of hunger and incurable diseases. Millions still live below the poverty line. Health care is still only available to a privileged few. Some nations around the world are still ruled by tyrants. Our technological progress has not necessarily enhanced our ethics and values. Christmas is still a lonely time for many.

While we are saddened by these issues, I imagine no one is more saddened by them than our Savior, no one more grieved than our Lord. He grieves not just because of the injustice we see in many social issues, though he does care about them. He grieves not just because of our economic inequities, though he does desire for all to prosper. He grieves not just because of the lack of ethics and values in our leaders, he desires and expects our leaders to be just. He grieves not just because of our loneliness, though he desires no one to be plagued by the pain of loneliness. He grieves in the knowledge that another Christmas season will come and go with many celebrating without the true knowledge of the full meaning of Christmas. Many will receive gifts, sing songs, and attend parties that will be centered on a cultural celebration rather than spiritual renewal.

In this season of Christmas, let us be resolved to bring a smile to our hearts and to the heart of our Savior; let us truly make it his birthday and give him a gift that is meaningful to him. Let us celebrate the true meaning of Christmas by renewing our commitment to be his hands and feet in our world. Let us ensure that no one feels alone this Christmas. Let us remind those around us of the Light that is within us: the true Light of Christmas. Let us allow our light to shine so brightly that they will desire to move from darkness to his Light. Let us allow his Light to shine in our workplace, in our communities, and in our homes. We may not be able to solve the social ills or the economic challenges overnight, we may not be able to solve all world hunger next week, and we may not be able to ensure that our leaders lead with courage and honor in every office, but one thing we can do is guarantee that those around us who are in darkness will see the great Light, the true Light of Christmas.

More than two thousand years ago, those who were in darkness saw a great Light—a transformative Light that has brought hope to all who have embraced it ever since. A Light so bright that it has not ceased to shine. This is the Light of the world, the hope of our day, the Savior of the world. No matter our lot in life, we can be assured of one thing: one day, because of this Light, everything will be restored. There will be no more hunger and poverty, no more sickness and disease, and no more tyranny and hatred. All wrongdoers will be judged, and we shall be with him forever. This is the hope of Christmas, the Light of the world.

Father, may you grant us the grace to see beyond our circumstances and limitations and place our hope in the coming of our Lord and the restoration of all things through your Son, Jesus Christ. Thank you, Lord, for the Light of world, the Son of God, and the Savior of our souls. Thank you for the gift of your Son, Jesus Christ, our Lord. Amen.

Patrice Tsague is the cofounder of the Nehemiah Project International Ministries and resides in Milwaukie, Oregon.

Fourth Friday of Advent

GAIL WEYERHAEUSER

EXODUS 23:1–9 · LUKE 1:57–66

On the eighth day they came to circumcise the child, and they were going to name him after his father Zechariah, but his mother spoke up and said, "No! He is to be called John."
LUKE 1:59–60

Truth Be Told

There is much in this passage that reflects normal, predictable human experience and emotions. A woman has a full-term pregnancy and delivers a healthy baby boy. It happens thousands of times a day all over the earth; thanksgiving is appropriate, but hardly noteworthy.

It is the unpredictable, unexpected events of this passage that capture our imagination and interest. God has stepped into human history. Events unfold that are beyond human explanation. A conception occurs for a couple thought too old. And the father's verbal ability is taken away when he doubts God's ability to bring a child of old age into being. The story grows more interesting. There is mystery, sacred mystery afoot. Who is this child and what do he and his birth mean? People are talking.

Then comes the naming. In Jewish tradition, circumcision and the naming of a male child occurred on the eighth day of life. Respect for the father was shown through naming the first male child after him. This also kept a lineage of unique names within separate tribes. It was understandable that everyone expected Elizabeth to affirm Zechariah as the baby's name. But the couple had obviously been communicating with each other about God's presence in this child's life. Elizabeth was firm and clear in stating the child's name was John. She appears at ease in asserting herself and in others looking to her for direction. It is interesting to ponder how the pregnancy had grown her faith and character.

Their community was ready for the predictable, but both Zechariah and Elizabeth knew there was nothing usual in the birth of this child. Zechariah was clear and strong in the uniqueness of this child's name. He was John. Then comes the final miracle in this passage. The community had assumed Zechariah's speech was gone forever, perhaps from a paralytic episode. But when he declared the truth of the child's name through writing, Zechariah's speech was restored. Truth will be spoken. The parents dramatically declared the uniqueness of God's work in their lives and in this child. The conception, pregnancy, and naming of this child were all outside the expected.

As humans, we love the predictable for our own lives. We want control. We want sure and easy outcomes. But complexities interrupt our contentment. We are faced with events and circumstances out of our control. Surprisingly, amazingly, it is often these unpredictable, out-of-our-control things that provide the true blessings in our lives and opportunities for growth. It is in the unpredictable, the not normal, and even in the hard times that God's presence and gifts are deeply felt.

Gracious Lord, grant each of us the grace to plan as we can, to manage as we are able, but also to let go and let you act as you wish and must. Amen.

Gail Toycen Weyerhaeuser works as a clinical psychologist in Tacoma, Washington, where she lives.

Fourth Saturday of Advent

STACEY WOMACK

JEREMIAH 7:1–7 · LUKE 2:25–32

Simeon took him in his arms and praised God, saying: "Sovereign Lord, as you have promised, you may now dismiss your servant in peace. For my eyes have seen your salvation, which you have prepared in the sight of all nations: a light for revelation to the Gentiles, and the glory of your people Israel."
LUKE 2:28–32

The Gift of Today

Can you imagine waiting hundreds of years for a Savior, only being able to decipher bits and pieces of God's plan? I wonder if it came as a surprise to Simeon, when he saw the Lord Christ, that he was only a baby.

I imagine that a reason why most Israelites were unable to recognize, or to accept, Jesus as the long-awaited Messiah was that they had their own ideas of how the Messiah would be revealed. They wanted him to appear on the scene in royal splendor to defeat their enemies. They expected a mighty display of power and glory, and they wanted their enemies finally dismayed and brought down. But God had other plans for their enemies, and the Messiah would operate unexpectedly for the healing of all.

We try to figure out how God should work things out in our lives, and we have convictions about how God ought to fix our problems. When things don't go as we think they should, we become disheartened. We think something is wrong or that God has failed us. But slowly, we learn how God has his own plans and ways of operating. It requires that we trust him and allow him to have the right to do things his way, rather than our way. I have come to conclude that if I can figure out how God is going to answer my prayer, then that is exactly how he will *not* answer it!

Not only do we assume that we know how God should act, making God too small, but also we feel that we must help him do his job. We try to manipulate our circumstances, and we worry that we should be doing something more than just praying. Because of this, we can miss all the ways God is blessing us. Sending his Son to be Immanuel, "God with us," was a gift. Because it was so unlike what they expected, many people missed it.

We can esteem Simeon, then, who had long trained himself in the ways of God—how God wanted to be rather than how his people preferred him to be. And one day, in the temple, it was Simeon who recognized the Messiah, and went forward to receive into his aged hands the Blessing his people had long hoped for.

We are really not much different from those living in the time of Jesus. We take a lot for granted. Every day we have food to eat, clothes to wear, a roof over our heads, but we miss how God is blessing our lives. We overlook, and fail to cherish that every day we wake up, and every breath we take, is a gift from God.

God, open my eyes to see the many ways you are blessing me. Help me not take for granted all the gifts you give me every day. Thank you for sending your Son to save me. Thank you for the ways you continue to save me each day and season of my life. Amen.

Stacey Womack is the founder and executive director of Abuse Recovery Ministry and Services and lives in Hillsboro, Oregon.

THE *Birth* OF THE *Christ Child*

Christmas Eve

PAUL ANDERSON

TITUS 3:4–7 · LUKE 2:1–7 · ISAIAH 16:5

But when the kindness and love of God our Savior appeared, he saved us, not because of righteous things we had done, but because of his mercy. He saved us through the washing of rebirth and renewal by the Holy Spirit, whom he poured out on us generously through Jesus Christ our Savior, so that, having been justified by his grace, we might become heirs having the hope of eternal life.
TITUS 3:4–7

The Journey That Changed the World

It's Christmas Eve—probably the most sacred evening of the year for most Christian families around the world—but how do you celebrate this day in your own home? Have you been working nonstop getting food together and the home ready for family time, or getting last-minute presents wrapped and under the tree? Or, have you been traveling to be with loved ones or striving to get to a Christmas Eve worship service on time? The challenge is to work through the busyness of the day to engage meaningfully in its central business—the celebration of Jesus' birth.

As we think of Mary and Joseph two millennia ago, they, too, were pressed from all sides. Luke explained in real historical context that their visit to Jerusalem was a factor of an earlier census and the later tax measures issued by the ruler of the day.

It reminds us that their lives, like ours, were full of pressures and cares.

These things help us understand more about the pressure that Joseph must have felt as he traveled that confusing and lonely journey. First, the wealth of Herod Archelaus (son of Herod the Great—banished because of his harsh crackdown on Jewish uprisings) was confiscated and used to support the Roman occupation of the region. Second, livestock and produce collections were replaced by the garnering of hard currency, making it much harder for farmers and herders to make their payments. This caused an uprising by Judas the Galilean—declaring that this new system of taxation amounted to enslavement, and the Romans stepped in and crucified two thousand Jewish men near Nazareth. Third, registering the populace allowed Romans to keep especially close track of leading men in society; later Roman authorities put to death known descendants of David so as to avert messianic uprisings.

In addition to feeling the oppression of Roman rule, with Mary's being pregnant and with no place to stay, the young couple must have felt terribly discouraged! But notice how things changed in the rest of Luke's story. First, a place of hospitality was provided, though modest and among the animals. Second, heavenly angels appeared to shepherds—the common folk of the land—connecting the lowly with the royal. Third, in worshiping the Christ-child, the chorus of the angels became the passion of the shepherds, too: "Glory to God in the highest heaven, and on earth peace to those on whom his favor rests" (Luke 2:14).

We are reminded through the realities of the pressures and challenges that Mary and Joseph felt on that Christmas Eve journey that God's purpose and plans are established in unlikely places and ways. On that first Christmas morn, the royal tent of King David was pitched in an animal shelter, and his inauguration was celebrated by peasants. But long after the rise and fall of the Roman Empire, the reign of the babe in a feeding trough continues. Of his kingdom there is no end, and "having been justified by his grace," we too become royal "heirs having the hope of eternal life." That is great news to celebrate this Christmas Eve, and every day in the year to come!

Blessed Lord, thank you for the gift of knowing about this journey that changes everything. We thank you for the courage of Joseph, the faith of Mary, and the grace of hospitality of the manger. This Christmas Eve, may we be assured of your companionship on the journey we are on. Amen.

Paul N. Anderson is a professor of biblical and Quaker studies at George Fox University in Newberg, Oregon, where he lives.

Christmas Day

EARL PALMER

PSALMS 103 · LUKE 2:8–20

And there were shepherds living out in the fields nearby, keeping watch over their flocks at night. An angel of the Lord appeared to them, and the glory of the Lord shone around them, and they were terrified.
LUKE 2:8–9

The Day Like No Other

Shepherds in the hill country of Judea were with their sheep. They needed to keep alert for dangers, especially at night. Saint Luke called them guards of the sheep. But these particular Judean guards were suddenly met with a great surprise. An angel of the Lord stood in front of them. They were terrified because of the shock and the light—glory shone around them. The angel told them, "Do not be afraid." Then what unfolded was this announcement: "I bring you good news of great joy for you and all people. It is news about the birth of a savior. News about the long expectation in Israel's history for the Lord's Messiah. He is now here! He is born in David's city." These shepherds were then invited to see for themselves the proof of this good news.

Then the angel was joined by a large company of heavenly troops. "Host" is the word in most texts, but the Greek word *stratios* is best translated "army."

This great army chorus sings the first Christmas carol. "Glory to God in the highest, and on Earth peace, goodwill toward men and women." "Goodwill" is the right word to translate *eudokia* (the most literal translation of this song would be "Glory to God in the highest, and on Earth peace to men and women; this is the good decision of God").

The shepherds went to Bethlehem and saw for themselves how this amazing news was true. When they found Mary, Joseph, and the infant Jesus, they told what they heard from the angel choir. Luke made one more reflection upon this Christmas Eve incident. We heard that Mary the mother of Jesus welcomed the shepherds' visit, and she "treasured up all these things and pondered them in her heart" (Luke 2:19).

The birth of Jesus according to the New Testament is a quiet event. There are no obvious public markers. Only two sets of visitors are invited by God the Father to witness the birth of Jesus: Matthew told of wise men from the East who were invited; these foreign visitors were looking for a king, and they found Jesus. Luke told of night-shift shepherds who, probably together with their sheep, went to see the holy family. The manger was just right for the family, their visitors, and the Son of God. These shepherds were invited because every birth needs witnesses, and not just anyone, but visitors at such a time who would have a calming and assuring presence with a young mother and her husband who were some ninety miles from their home in Nazareth.

Why are the shepherds so important for our understanding of Christmas? It is because they are historical signposts for us along with Caesar Augustus, who was emperor when the census was ordered. These historical witnesses heard about the joyous good news that love came down to Earth, and they experienced a measurable sign. That sign is very significant: "in David's City, you will find a child." This they did, and we now have their human witness that love is not an idea or ideal, but a person. The shepherds were first to see it. No wonder Mary treasured their visit. Their presence was a concrete validation of that moment in her own life when the angel Gabriel met a young woman and told her mysterious words—"You will conceive and give birth to a son, and you are to call him Jesus" (Luke 1:31). I wonder if they sang the song that the army chorale sang to them and that we have been singing ever since.

Gracious and loving God, we thank you for the many ways you remind us of the specialness of this day. Like the shepherds and wise men, may we bow down and worship the newborn King. May we rise up and go into our world and like the angels proclaim, "Glory be the newborn King." Amen.

Earl Palmer is the founder of Earl Palmer Ministries in Seattle, Washington, where he lives.

THE *Twelve Days* OF *Christmas*

Introduction to the Twelve Days of Christmas

Fr. Rick Ganz

ISAIAH 62:6–12 · LUKE 2:8–20

The Twelve Days of Christmas—It's About Time

When economic considerations prevail, Christmas is about the time set aside for buying and selling of stuff for Christmas. We who shop are given (by whom?) each year more time to shop; we who sell need more time to get our companies into the black. In this frame of reference, time is made to serve things . . . as we, in turn, are drawn into serving them too.

But this is not what time is for in relation to people. Abraham Heschel wrote in his famous essay The Sabbath, "To have more [stuff] does not mean to be more [of a person]."[6] He also wrote: "The higher goal of spiritual living is not to amass a wealth of [content, stuff], but to face sacred moments."[7]

For people, time itself is the gift, in which timeless experiences happen, such as the birth of a child, of our Savior, our Reconciler, of our God-with-us. At Christmas we don't need time, or need to insist that we be given more time. Rather, we take time. Again, Heschel wrote: "We must not forget that it is not a thing that lends significance to a moment; it is the moment that lends significance to things."[8]

For animals, as far as we can guess, time governs them, drives them, and gets defined by their instinctual patterns of life: mating season, migration season, etc. The economic world constantly seeks to put the personal world under the patterning and bondage of (too little) time. But for people, we can, and should, in significant measure govern time: it is our time; we take time, and we even say (and this is very interesting) that we make time for what matters to us.

Consider a popular, nonreligious song associated with the Christmas season: "The Twelve Days of Christmas."

The song narrates the story of a remarkable quantity of stuff having been given someone over the course of twelve days. Through the use of a twelvefold repetition, the "thing" shown to be of most significant value to the author is that "my true love gave [these gifts] to me." The song reminds us to take time to notice the one who loves him or her, and his or her great and generous giving of him- or herself, in whose grace one would delight to dwell timelessly.

When each new gift is received, then each and all of the previous gifts are named again, and remembered in the order in which they were received—from last to first. Only a person who loves the Giver will remember his or her gifts so artfully, and with such perfect recall.

When have we taken time, in even a single day of our lives, to remember so well the gifts that we have received, and from whom?

The tradition of the church stipulates that between Christmas Eve and Twelfth Night (the eve of the feast of the Epiphany) we take time to step out of time's dominion as economic selves and to dwell as personal selves who know that we are loved truly, and given much, and to make time for those who love us, and whom we love. It's about time.

Fr. Rick Ganz, SJ, has been a Jesuit and Roman Catholic priest for forty years, and is a teacher, writer, and spiritual director residing in Portland, Oregon.

First Day of Christmas

KEITH HAMILTON

PSALMS 98 · 1 JOHN 4:7–11

Dear friends, let us love one another, for love comes from God. Everyone who loves has been born of God and knows God. Whoever does not love does not know God, because God is love. This is how God showed his love among us: He sent his one and only Son into the world that we might live through him. This is love: not that we loved God, but that he loved us and sent his Son as an atoning sacrifice for our sins. Dear friends, since God so loved us, we also ought to love one another.

1 JOHN 4:7–11

It's a Wonderful Life

Who doesn't love a great Christmas movie? Our family favorite is *It's a Wonderful Life*. It follows the life of George Bailey, who starts out trying to lasso the moon with his wild dreams. When the stock market crash of 1929 hits, he loses almost everything that he has built up over his life. So discouraged, he prays a simple prayer that God answers through George's guardian angel, Clarence. He then makes a terrible wish—that he had never been born—and *whoosh*; it is answered!

In the vision given him of a world into which he had never been born, all he knew to be real was gone—his job, his family, his house. You see, the town of Bedford Falls looked much different because George had never been born to form it. Because he had not existed, he had no family; there were no kids called

Bailey. He beheld his wife, who was instead a spinster librarian, who had never found a good man to marry. The Bailey Family Savings and Loan never happened either, because he was not there to lead it. Homes were never built because no funds were loaned to needy families. His brother, Harry, was lying in the local cemetery because George had not been there to rescue him when he fell through the ice as a young child.

This vision of an alternate reality was horrible; and he longed for release from this dark vision and a return to his real life, even with all of its problems. He again prayed to God to have his old life back, and—*whoosh!*—everything he had known and loved was back! What rejoicing there was in the Bailey home that Christmas Eve in 1929. You see, George received the greatest gift ever—getting to live his life again to the fullest.

First John 4 reminds us that Jesus really did come because of *love*, because of unconditional love. Verse 8 declares that God is love! And verse 9 goes further to tell us *how* that love was given to us at Christmas—God sent his only Son into the world so that we can live through him. Jesus came and lived and died so that we could see life differently—much as George Bailey did when his life was returned to him.

Have you ever given consideration to the thought of what our world would be like without Jesus' birth—if he had never been born? And we wonder what our life, each of our lives, would be without the grace and beauty of Jesus given in this world. And we consider during this holy season whether we accurately perceive how Jesus has made a difference in our lives, personally, God with us. We ponder what Truth would mean if Jesus had no part of what Truth means.

Because I have spent the greater part of my life in an academic setting, where homework is the way toward a deeper understanding of a subject, I invite all of us to take time to ponder more that *love* is God's reason for sending his Son. Do we understand this deeply enough, and do we grasp the real difference Christ's coming has made in our lives?

Lord, I cannot go through Christmas without affirming again that you **did** *come, that you were born, and that my life is profoundly different today because of your active relationship with me. Help me to experience Christmas through the biblical account of your actual coming out of* **love**. *In the name of Jesus the Baby I pray. Amen.*

Dr. Keith Hamilton is the founding president of Alaska Christian College and lives in Soldotna, Alaska.

Second Day of Christmas

HOLLEN FRAZIER

PSALM 147:1–6 · JOHN 3:16–21

The Lord sustains the humble but casts the wicked to the ground.
PSALM 147:6

"Whoever believes in him is not condemned, but whoever does not believe stands condemned already because they have not believed in the name of God's one and only Son."
JOHN 3:18

"But whoever lives by the truth comes into the light, so that it may be seen plainly that what they have done has been in the sight of God."
JOHN 3:21

Walking in His Light

Walking in belief means to move forward with the light of Jesus Christ shining in my heart. With him, I do not walk as condemned, but as forgiven and set free. As I walk in the Light, he guides each step I take, bringing me into his presence with unfailing grace.

But in this life, it is easy to fall prey to pride's temptation, relying on myself and believing that my understanding and wisdom are enough for me. However, I have learned that to seek such a path of independence from God is unwise.

During this Christmas season, I find my hope strengthened through the miracle of Jesus' birth. When God sent us his precious Son, he brought Light into the world. And I notice, as a director of an orphan care ministry, this Light of Christ in the eyes of each child whom I welcome and help. At times, the orphan crisis of our world seems unceasing to me. However, when I see the light in the eyes of those children, I grow in confidence that God is accomplishing a divine purpose even in these hopeless circumstances. If I cling to him, then I am free from fear, despair, and doubt.

When I do not trust in God's sovereignty over the life of an orphan who needs a family or a school to attend, I walk in darkness and am unable to see. When I neglect to cry out to God for a greater understanding of how he is at work for these children, I become frustrated with my own hidden sins and shame. I begin to fall into a pit that my own self-reliance has dug, in which place I forget that Jesus' life is sufficient, that Jesus is enough. Isn't that what each of us remembers at Christmas—that "the Light who has come into the world" is all we need? Even one ray of that Light can dispel the darkest dark.

Molly was six years old when I first met her in a Bulgarian orphanage. I saw her only a handful of times during the year when her adoption was being finalized. When I first saw her precious face, I reached down and physically hugged her. Years later, Molly contacted me, and she told me how that one hug was a life-changing experience for her. She said that she held on to that love, that Light. Today, she is twenty-one, and she lives in Washington.

At Christmas, we celebrate the birth of Jesus—God wrapped in swaddling clothes. Through the Light of a baby brought into the world so long ago, I can today serve children who need hope, who need love, who need a relationship with Jesus. The moment each one of these humble children is sustained through a physical touch, a lovingly prepared meal, or by the gift of clothing, it is as if God himself sends his Light through these acts of love. Although the gift may be small, the outcome can be big. It may be only one shaft of Light that is needed for a person to be able to see Christ.

Father of Lights, we humbly praise you this day as we kneel in your radiant presence. We ask for more of your Light in the dark corners of our soul. Seek out the places that we keep hidden from you, so that your holiness can grow within us. Go before us in our lives and works and lead us in all that we do. Thank you for being the Light who lives inside us, and for sending your precious Son to Earth as a baby. Amen.

Hollen Frazier serves as the executive director of All God's Children International and lives in Camas, Washington.

Third Day of Christmas

Jim Schmotzer

PSALMS 74:1–10 · LUKE 12:35–37

"Be dressed ready for service and keep your lamps burning, like servants waiting for their master to return from a wedding banquet, so that when he comes and knocks they canimmediately open the door for him. It will be good for those servants whose master finds them watching when he comes."
Luke 12:35–37

Inbreaking

The Advent season, with calendars and rituals, is focused on preparation and readiness for the coming Christmas Day. But maybe there is another message, the message of getting and being ready for that which is unknown and unpredictable. In focus and preparation for the coming of Christ on Christmas, we may miss the intervention of God in the midst of our waiting. Advent and Christmas are events and dates we have determined and scheduled. Reflection shows me that God has yet to be bound by my expectations or human time systems. Christian Wiman helped us understand this when he said, "Inbreaking is the theological term for Christ's appearance in the world and in our lives—there is no coaxing it, no way to earn it, no way to prepare except to hone your capacity to respond, which is, finally, your capacity to experience life and death."[9]

God has a habit of showing up when least expected and yet when most needed. At times God whispers in the dark or shouts in the crowd. God, and the awareness of the presence of God, is not limited to times of solitude and meditative reflection or gatherings of ceremony and worship. God has been known to show up in the midst of a family argument, in the laughter of conversation at mealtime, in the exhaustion of caring for a sick loved one in the middle of the night, in the fear of financial struggles, and in a moment of shared surprise meeting and conversation in the grocery store.

One perspective is that God shows up when the time is right, in special ways. I believe the simpler reality is that God is always present, and that the showing up is more about our awareness of the reality of him being with us. And maybe that is the challenge and gift of being ready.

We do well in this Christmas season to open ourselves to God's faithful and special presence rather than seeking to control or manipulate God from our feeble perspective. Our times are in his hands.

Holy God, thankfully you are not bound by our
schedules and systems.
Help us to be ready to meet you in the moment,
Any moment,
And enjoy the gift of your presence
In times of plenty and want.
Amen.

Jim Schmotzer serves as a coach and consultant through Jim Schmotzer & Associates in Bellingham, Washington, where he lives.

Fourth Day of Christmas

HEATHER TUININGA

ISAIAH 30:21 · 2 PETER 1:17

Whether you turn to the right or to the left, your ears will hear a voice behind you, saying, "This is the way; walk in it."
ISAIAH 30:21

Walk in the Love

Are you spending this day reflecting on the past year as it comes to a close, and do you find yourself wishing that you had made some different choices? Or are you already looking toward the year ahead with hope and optimism about what it may bring?

Whether we are looking back or looking forward, we may find in today's biblical verses things that will illuminate this special day in Christmastide that the Lord has given us to live.

I have read Isaiah 30:21 many times, and each time I have found it confusing. Does it mean that no matter which way we choose to go, God will endorse that direction? If that were so, then what does Matthew 7:14, "Small is the gate and narrow the road that leads to life, and only a few find it" mean? I am often left wondering how to find the small gate and narrow road, not knowing whether it is to the right or to the left.

So, this time when I read that text, I decided to consult some other translations of it, seeing what I might find to lessen my confusion about its meaning. It was in The Living Bible translation that I found this way of expressing the thought: "And if you leave God's paths and go astray, you will hear a voice behind you say, 'No, this is the way; walk here'" (TLB).

Now, that makes much more sense. Regardless of what the people of Israel had done (which is spelled out in verses 1–17), if they would listen for God's voice, then he would get them back on the right path. God was calling them to repentance, rest, quietness, and trust (v. 15), and he is calling us also to the same narrow road.

As we reflect on the past year, the good news is that no matter how far off track we have wandered, if we listen for God's voice, he will guide us back to the right path for us. And as we look out to the year ahead, we can again listen to God's voice and the words he said about Jesus after his baptism and at the transfiguration: "This is my beloved Son, and I am wonderfully pleased with him" (Matt. 3:17; 17:5 TLB).

As sons and daughters of God and coheirs with Christ (see Romans 8:14–17), our Father in heaven is also saying these words about us. We are his beloved sons and daughters, in whom he is well pleased. May God's unconditional love infuse all of our thoughts and plans for the year ahead.

Holy Lord God, we ask you to forgive us for the ways that we have gone astray this past year. Help us to hear and trust your voice as you guide us into the year ahead, and continually remind us to rest in the reality of your unconditional love for us, your sons and daughters. Amen.

Heather Tuininga is a senior associate and oversees philanthropic advising services for Marigold Associates in Seattle, Washington, where she lives.

Fifth Day of Christmas

Gerard Long

ISAIAH 62 · MARK 11:23–26

As a bridegroom rejoices over his bride,
so will your God rejoice over you.
Isaiah 62:5

"Truly I tell you, if anyone says to this mountain, 'Go, throw yourself into the sea,' and does not doubt in their heart but believes that what they say will happen, it will be done for them. Therefore I tell you, whatever you ask for in prayer, believe that you have received it, and it will be yours. And when you stand praying, if you hold anything against anyone, forgive them, so that your Father in heaven may forgive you your sins."
Mark 11:23–25

The Blessed Hope

During the season of Advent, we look forward to, "while we wait for the blessed hope—the appearing of the glory of our great God and Savior, Jesus Christ" (Titus 2:13). What a great day that will be! Then we will see how much God loves us. The parting will be over and the party can begin—the wedding feast of the Lamb!

Isaiah 62:5 tells us that, "as a bridegroom rejoices over a bride, so will your God rejoice over you" Oh, how great is the love that God has for us! Jesus, we're told, will present us to the Father "without fault and with great joy" (Jude 24).

But for now, while we patiently wait for Jesus' second coming, there is work to do. God has posted us as watchmen. And what is it that the watchmen are called to do? Isaiah 62:7 tells us we're to give God "no rest" until he establishes his kingdom on earth. In other words, God is calling his children to be people of prayer and to come to him continually (1 Thess. 5:17) with requests that "your kingdom come, your will be done, on earth as it is in heaven" (Matt. 6:10).

Jesus told us in our second passage how we're supposed to pray—with belief in our hearts. This isn't belief that we can move the mountain, but it's faith in God, that he is in control and is working everything out for his good pleasure. As our faith in God grows, largely through the painful or difficult experiences in our lives, we become bolder and more persistent and expectant in our prayers.

The mountain is any challenge or concern you are facing in your life. God really does want us to give him no rest over every burden we carry for a lost relative, friend, or colleague. Or, maybe you have a health issue or a concern over a relationship or a financial issue. God wants you to give him no rest until his kingdom comes and his will is done in the situation you are bringing to him.

Through belief in Jesus Christ and his death and resurrection, we have access to God's throne of grace and provision for our every need and concern (Heb. 4:16). I encourage you this Advent to go boldly to God with your concerns and burdens and give him no rest until he establishes his kingdom. But when you go, make sure there is no one you need to forgive from your heart (Mark 11:25)! As we walk through this season of Christmas, it is a great moment to reaffirm and practice forgiveness just as God has forgiven you through Jesus' sacrifice on the cross. Let us be known as generously forgiving people!

Oh, great God, thank you once again for my precious Lord and Savior, Jesus Christ. Thank for the wonderful hope of his second coming, and please help me to live expectantly for that great day. Please fill me afresh today with your Holy Spirit, and help me to be faithful to your calling on my life. Lord, please help me to understand that you have prepared work for me to do, to bring in your kingdom. Draw me ever closer into your presence, and teach me to cast all my concerns and burdens on you. I surrender myself again to you, Lord, and I ask that you help me to receive your mercy and grace. Search my heart, and show me if there is anyone I need to forgive. Just as you have forgiven me, I choose to live a life of forgiveness. I love you, Lord, and I ask all these things in Jesus' name. Amen.

Gerard Long serves as the executive director for Alpha USA and lives with his wife in Chicago, Illinois.

Sixth Day of Christmas

JOSEPH CASTLEBERRY

EXODUS 3:1–6 · LUKE 2:41–51

God called to him . . . "Moses! Moses!" And Moses said, "Here I am." "Do not come any closer," God said. ". . . the place where you are standing is holy ground. . . . I am the God of your father, the God of Abraham, the God of Isaac and the God of Jacob." At this, Moses hid his face, because he was afraid to look at God.
EXODUS 3:4–6

Moses, Mary, and a Message

Heroes pondering mysteries—Moses marveled over a burning bush that fire does not consume, and Mary treasured in her heart the precocious wisdom of her child Jesus before the eminent teachers of the temple in Jerusalem. The stories speak with special relevance at this season that stirs the hearts of believers to dwell on the mysteries of God.

As Moses contemplated the burning bush, God called to him and Moses responded, "Here I am." God then warned him, "Do not come any closer . . . You are standing [on] holy ground." The *mysterium tremendum* descended on Moses, and he hid his face, afraid to look at the terrible holiness of God. As Rudolf Otto wrote in *The Idea of the Holy*, human beings have always responded to the Holy One in fear. When angels proclaiming the Messiah's birth appeared to shepherds watching over their flocks by night in Luke 2:9, we read that they were terrified.

Mary's experience of the Holy stands out. When God's angel appeared to her, he urged her not to be afraid (Luke 1:30), assuring her of God's favor and promising that the Holy Spirit would come upon her, that the power of the Most High would overshadow her. As a result, she would give birth to a holy child called "the Son of God." Like Moses, she responded, "[Here] I am" (Luke 1:38), God filled her with the Spirit and worked a miracle in her womb.

Afterward, the holy child was born—worshiped by shepherds, acknowledged in the temple by the holy elders Anna and Simeon, and later celebrated when "everyone who heard him was amazed at his understanding and his answers" (Luke 2:47). Mary treasured these things in her heart, deeply touched by the faithfulness of God.

God's visitation to us in Christ brought clarity and wonder to that which Moses received. God calls us closer. Because of what the Father sent in Christ—perfect reconciliation between God and humanity—and because Christ sent the Holy Spirit at Pentecost—an abiding fullness of God's presence with us—we receive the full expression of the invitation that Moses experienced. God has come to us, once and for all. Unlike the visitors and teachers at the temple who heard the wisdom of the Christ child once, we can hear God's Word every day in the Scriptures through the illumination of the Spirit who powerfully dwells in us.

We treasure in our hearts, as Mary did, the words and deeds of the Savior. They are a promise that has been fulfilled and one that shall fill our days and all days to come.

Father, today we draw close to Christ, responding to the mysterious treasure of your invitation and visitation. May we be filled with your Spirit, with wonder and awe. And may we be continually sanctified by your holy presence through all our days. In Jesus' name, amen.

Dr. Joseph Castleberry is the president of Northwest University in Kirkland, Washington, where he lives.

Seventh Day of Christmas

Fr. Steve Sundborg

PSALM 111 · 1 THESSALONIANS 2:1–5

Praise the Lord. I will extol the Lord with all my heart
in the council of the upright and in the assembly.
Psalm 111:1

The Practice of Gratitude

On this day in Christmastide, when we look back on the past year and forward to the New Year, it is helpful to examine our daily attitudes in the light of our Christian faith. Rather than looking back with regret for what we did not do and looking forward with resolution for an impossibly different new year, we can see the past and the future in a new way as inspired by the psalmist. He calls us to live with a unique kind of gratitude—rather than with regret or resolution: "I will extol the Lord with my whole heart."

The most important decision we make every morning is whether we will choose to live that day grudgingly or gratefully. The grudging way is to bemoan how busy we are, to focus on the difficult things we must face or the difficult people we must deal with, and to approach the day miserly, trying to wrest from it a few moments of peace, privacy, or relaxation. The grateful way to approach the day is to be glad for life itself, to relish our faith that gives such meaning to every day of life, and to look forward to God's gifts of the surprises of the day and the rich array of people we will encounter. How we approach each day is a choice. The grateful way is a choice supported by God's grace: "I will extol the Lord with my whole heart."

The psalmist invites us not just to give thanks but to give thanks with our whole hearts. Rare is the life that does not have some thankfulness in it. However, it is only to the Lord that we can give thanks with our whole hearts. Only God is capable of opening us so that the whole of our hearts give thanks. Only to God belongs our whole gratitude. George Basil Hume said, "Judgment is whispering into the ear of a merciful and compassionate God the story of my life as I have never been able to tell anyone."[10] Only God is big enough and knows us well enough that we can give thanks to him alone with our whole hearts. The choice to live with this kind of thankfulness is not a resolution, but is made possible by God's love and grace and must flow from our daily prayer.

If while praying each morning, we choose with God's grace to give thanks in this way, we will be extending the gift of Christmas every day of our lives and will bring grateful hearts to the congregation that praises God.

Gracious and generous God, create in each of us a clean and full heart that recognizes the daily ways you bless and keep us. May we go into this day with words and deeds that honor you and bless the world in which we live, work, and play. Amen.

Fr. Stephen V. Sundborg, SJ, is a Roman Catholic priest and president of Seattle University in Seattle, Washington, where he lives.

Eighth Day of Christmas

Kim Porter

JOSHUA 1:9 · LUKE 2:36–40

"Have I not commanded you? Be strong and courageous. Do not be afraid; do not be discouraged, for the Lord your God will be with you wherever you go."
Joshua 1:9

There was also a prophet, Anna, the daughter of Penuel, of the tribe of Asher. She was very old; she had lived with her husband seven years after her marriage, and then was a widow until she was eighty-four. She never left the temple but worshiped night and day, fasting and praying. Coming up to them at that very moment, she gave thanks to God and spoke about the child to all who were looking forward to the redemption of Jerusalem. When Joseph and Mary had done everything required by the Law of the Lord, they returned to Galilee to their own town of Nazareth. And the child grew and became strong; he was filled with wisdom, and the grace of God was on him.
Luke 2:36–40

Looking Forward!

What are you looking forward to? It may be tempting to give a pat answer to this question as we consider our hopes and our plans for this new year, or we may recognize the importance of the question and become more reflective about it. We may consider, for example, the value of having a healthier lifestyle, of committing more time to be with friends and family, or of resolving to learn something new. In our Advent/Christmas time of year, it is good to pause and to linger over our hopes and plans, exploring the possibility of them and feeling for their source in the deeper parts of our souls.

What are you looking forward to? In Luke 2:36–40, we get to watch a woman's commitment to the depth of this question, and how it caused her to recognize him for whom she had waited.

As the scene opens, we find Joseph and Mary in the temple, to which they came to consecrate their firstborn son to the Lord. Their act of obedience to the law's command is what generations of Jewish parents have done before them. There was nothing but ordinary in what they did. Yet others, who knew for whom they hoped, recognized that someone not ordinary had come into the temple that day, and they looked down into the face of the Christ Child in Mary's arms.

It was a prophetess, Anna by name, who was prompted by the Spirit to join the intimate group that had gathered around a mother and father and their baby boy. As the light of a star had directed the Magi to the Child, so the prophetess Anna is a light here, illuminating what was hidden in the ordinary, shedding light on the presence of the Messiah. She lifts up her voice and shares life-changing news with anyone who will listen.

Anna speaks out of her own journey of waiting, of knowing for whom she hoped. She is a widow who finds a child, a prophetess who has spent many years in worship and prayer in the temple. Her vigilant pursuit of God, calling out day and night, has sharpened her awareness of God and of her people's need for redemption. She incarnates the longing of her people, and her life is the question: What are you looking forward to?

For God to come,
To end the silence and speak a word,
To set us free.

The fruit of Anna's God-centered life was that she had eyes to see the movements of God in the world. Thirty years before Jesus emerged into his public life and ministry, Anna had grasped already who he was and what he would accomplish. She recognized Immanuel, or "God with us," who came into the world to bring redemption and hope.

What was the response to Anna's words that day? We know that Jesus' mother pondered these matters with Joseph. But did the community imitate Anna's act of heartfelt praise for this Child, or did they continue on with their religious activity blind to God's presence? We do not know. But will we today heed Anna's call to take a second look at this Child and begin to recognize God in our very midst.

What are you looking forward to? It takes courage to take seriously this question and to answer it. We are invited to follow Anna's example by knowing for whom we hope, spending time in prayer and worship, while we await the movements of God to unfold in our lives.

Grant me, Lord, the strength and courage this day to
wait upon you, trusting in your redemptive power.
Help me to have eyes to see your movements of grace.
Amen.

Kim Porter serves as the vice president and director of Learning and Talent for InterVarsity Christian Fellowship and currently lives in Madison, Wisconsin.

Ninth Day of Christmas

KEN BEEBE

PSALM 8:3–9 · COLOSSIANS 4:2–6

When I consider your heavens, the work of your fingers, the moon and the stars, which you have set in place, what is mankind that you are mindful of them, human beings that you care for them?
PSALM 8:3–4

Devote yourselves to prayer, being watchful and thankful. And pray for us, too, that God may open a door for our message, so that we may proclaim the mystery of Christ, for which I am in chains. Pray that I may proclaim it clearly, as I should.
COLOSSIANS 4:2–4

Joyfully Devoted to Prayer

Paul's council to "devote yourselves to prayer" sometimes overwhelms me. I get discouraged, feeling that I am not able to measure up to the task. Instead of basking in the joy of prayer, prayer itself becomes an onerous obligation, a demand to work harder.

But the reality is that prayer is an immense privilege. Prayer stands at the very core of what it means to be in relationship with God. Is it not amazing that the God who created the universe is actually interested in interacting with you and me, going so far as to become human and to learn from the inside what we are like? Nowhere is this better articulated than in Psalm 8.

A long time ago, when I was a high-school student, Richard J. Foster spoke memorably about this psalm, preaching a sermon about it at summer camp. His insights have remained with me even to now. In his sermon, Foster asked the tallest boy in camp (who stood perhaps six foot six) to come stand next to him on the stage. This teen towered over the preacher.

Foster then stated that it would take 192 copies of this young man stacked atop each other to reach the height of the Empire State Building. He said that it would take 33,446 copies of the Empire State Building lined up to span the diameter of earth. And, he continued, if we took 11,740 Earths and set them side by side, that chain would reach the sun. And more startling still, he said that we would need to duplicate the Earth-to-sun journey 64,544 times to have traveled the distance between our galaxy and the next nearest star. Further, he noted that our galaxy, the Milky Way, contains about 100 billion stars, yet the Milky Way is just one of the 500 billion galaxies that we have so far been able to identify.

Foster concluded his sermon by quoting these lines from Psalm 8: "When I consider your heavens, the work of your fingers, the moon and the stars, which you have set in place, what is mankind that you are mindful of them, human beings that you care for them?"

Understood in this context, prayer becomes pretty special. What a gift from God! What a blessing that God allows us to bring to him our thoughts, our greatest joys, our deepest hurts, our struggles with sin, our concerns for friends and family members, our fears and aspirations.

Compared to Earth's 7 billion other human inhabitants, we each are so infinitesimally insignificant! We cannot fathom why God is willing to communicate individually with us, and to do so continually. He encourages us to *devote* ourselves to talking with him, and implies that he actually enjoys these interactions! He even shows interest in the most mundane aspects of our lives that even our closest friends may find boring. He loves us. He cares for us. He offers us hope. He provides wisdom, guidance, and the means to be the people he has designed us to be. And he delights in our heartfelt expressions of thanksgiving.

In this light, prayer becomes less a burden, and more a great blessing. So let us let go of discouragement and devote ourselves to prayer. Let us with confidence pour out our hearts' concerns to Jesus.

Lord God, we are amazed that you take joy in interacting with us; that you love us, care for us, and that you give yourself to us in love. Please come alongside us in this special season of grace, providing encouragement, hope, instruction, and a newfound joy in your gift of prayer. In the name of Jesus we pray. Amen.

Ken Beebe is the executive director of Twin Rocks Friends Camp and Conference Center in Rockaway Beach, Oregon, where he lives.

Tenth Day of Christmas

10

RANDY WOODLEY

ISAIAH 61:1–11 · LUKE 4:14–28

The Spirit of the Sovereign Lord is on me, because the Lord has anointed me to proclaim good news to the poor. He has sent me to bind up the brokenhearted, to proclaim freedom for the captives and release from darkness for the prisoners, to proclaim the year of the Lord's favor and the day of vengeance of our God, to comfort all who mourn.
Isaiah 61:1–2

Learning to See the Gift of the Common

By this time in his earthly life (Luke 4:14–28), Jesus knew that his life's mission was that of the Messiah. When he spoke in the synagogue that day among his close relatives and friends, Jesus made the startling claim that Isaiah's prophecy was now fulfilled! Every expectation the people had of the Messiah was now to be placed on Jesus' shoulders. Freedom, healing, justice, salvation, restoration, Jubilee, including the restoration of shalom, was now to be fulfilled in Jesus. But they did not believe him. And if we are honest with ourselves, neither do we!

Jesus' friends and family in Nazareth did not expect that God would answer their hope for the Messiah in the way that God chose to answer it, and especially by picking one of their own neighbors as Messiah. This act of God was too close to home, and too uncomfortable, for them to accept easily. It is easy to imagine someone in Nazareth saying, "Not through *that* family!" And yet Jesus was God, working to bring about a vision of peace and restoration.

Too often we simply do not perceive the way God moves among us and in the most common of ways. We often ask God to act in *uncommon* ways and miss that God often prefers to act in common ways. I wonder whether we could learn to be happy finding Jesus at work in the common things, such as finding God through words of encouragement offered us by a neighbor, or visiting someone in an elder care facility, or in the song of a bird, or by causing justice to be done for the oppressed.

Perhaps one of the reasons Jesus' great announcement proclaiming his messianic mission was made at his hometown synagogue was because God wanted to demonstrate how much we overlook the obvious. We sometimes get concerned about who is delivering the message, or how, and completely miss the message itself. Jesus' message was that God was fulfilling his promise to bring about a just and loving world in the midst of oppression, sickness, marginalization, and inequality. God's *shalom* is not utopian; it comes in fits and starts in this life, but through which we can have a glimpse of the next life. Sometimes, we get a longer glimpse of it. Sometimes, as it was for the people of Nazareth, shalom is living right next door to us, and still we miss it.

Jesus that day challenged his hometown community. He needed them to understand how they had missed seeing God at work. He chose to demonstrate to them how their own sense of ethnic superiority had made them blind to God's work among people that they had marginalized. Later, he demonstrated this when he worked through a Canaanite woman and a Syrian man. Both of those groups formerly had been oppressors of the Jews, yet Jesus extended them divine mercy. God has no favorites. In the end, most of those in his hometown of Nazareth did not believe him.

Sometimes it takes a great deal of discomfort to move us beyond our set ideas, especially our religious dictums. Jesus is always pushing us, not only to see the other (the common, the marginalized, the downtrodden), but to see how he is always at work among us, and in others.

As we reflect in this holy season on him who was born in the most common of circumstances, can we pause from our own prejudices, even religious ideals, and prepare our hearts for what God is actually doing around us? What will it take for us to notice Jesus in the most unexpected places and voices today?

Lord, God of the Unexpected, give us each the grace in this holy season of Christmas to be available to the ways that you surprise us when you love those whom we do not even notice, when you extend mercy to those who do not deserve it, and when you tell us the truth in the Scriptures. Grant us the capacity to let you be who you wish to be, and to act as you desire. Teach us your ways, O God. Amen.

Randy Woodley is the founder of Eagle's Wings Ministry and lives in Newberg, Oregon.

Eleventh Day of Christmas

Jeff and Terra Mattson

Psalm 28:7–10 · John 1:1–5

The Lord is my strength and my shield; my heart trusts in him, and he helps me. My heart leaps for joy, and with my song I praise him. The Lord is the strength of his people, a fortress of salvation for his anointed one. Save your people and bless your inheritance; be their shepherd and carry them forever.
Psalm 28:7–9

Who Do You Say That I Am?

Identity. Eight letters aligned to form a word that carries so much weight. Identity speaks to who we are, who we see ourselves as, and who others perceive us to be. In just eight letters, we are suddenly confronted with the totality of our essence! Merriam-Webster defines it in a way you may not have thought of: "the qualities, beliefs, etc., that make a particular person or group different from others." In other words, *our identity separates us.*

In Mark 8, Jesus asked his disciples what the word on the street was about him. This is not the first or only time that Jesus asked this question. The gospels of Mark (8:27–30) and Matthew (16:13–20) tell the same story. Luke recorded that Jesus was in the middle of a private prayer meeting when he raised the question with his disciples (9:18–21). John took us to the edges of the Jordan, where John the Baptist would have his own identity questioned (1:19–34), moments before Jesus stepped into the scene.

Identity was absolutely important to Jesus. More than anyone, he knew who he was and whom he was representing. Why then did he ask this question of his disciples?

Jesus was on mission to ensure that his disciples understood that he was the source of their identity. In following Jesus, the Twelve would separate themselves from others by identifying with Christ. Knowing him as "the Son of the living God," as Matthew wrote (16:16), would later give them the strength and hope to stand and face the opposition that would soon come. Do you feel opposition for identifying with Christ today?

The disciples reported that people were saying that he was a prophet. But then Jesus goes for the jugular. "Who do you say I am?" Simon Peter replied first, which does not surprise those of us who know Peter. Peter did not always get it right, but this time he nailed it like an Olympic ice skater sticking the triple axel. "You are the Messiah."

Where were you were when you first believed, as Peter did at that moment? How old were you? Who was with you? You knew that you knew that Jesus was the Christ, the Son of the living God, and no one or anything could take that away from you, right? But how did Peter know with such certainty? How did you know in that moment? That knowledge was and remains a gift from God! In truth, is there anything that you have achieved of eternal significance apart from God's hand?

After nailing his Olympic moment, Peter would later choke in his denial of Jesus. And yet, Jesus remained faithful to Peter, even entrusting to him the keys to the kingdom of heaven. Just as was Peter, so we in Christ are humbled yet secure; weak yet empowered.

What about you? If Jesus asked, "Who do you say that I am?" what would you say?

Lord, I praise your name: Jesus, the Christ, and the one I long for. For you are good and your love endures forever. Your faithfulness continues through all generations. Help me to keep you at the center of my identity, living my life according to you being Christ, my Messiah. Amen. (adapted from Ps. 100:4–5)

Jeff and Terra Mattson lead Living Wholehearted in Tualatin, Oregon, where they live.

Twelfth Day of Christmas

Greg Pennoyer

ISAIAH 9:2–7 · 1 TIMOTHY 4:1–5

For everything God created is good, and nothing is to be rejected if it is received with thanksgiving, because it is consecrated by the word of God and prayer.
1 Timothy 4:4–5

The Startling Reality of the Flesh

The Feast of the Epiphany, the final day of the Christmas season, has been celebrated by Christians since the third century. Although today it is almost forgotten compared to the festivities leading up to Christmas, Epiphany was so important to the early church that it predated the inclusion of Christmas Day (the Feast of the Nativity) in the church calendar.

I've often wondered why Epiphany meant so much to the early church, as well as what it might mean for us today. Part of the answer, I think, is suggested by Epiphany's relationship to the season of which it is the culmination. Isaiah's grand anthem in today's reading hints at this connection to the nativity, declaring, "For to us a child is born, to us a son is given, and the government will be on his shoulders. And he will be called Wonderful Counselor,

Mighty God, Everlasting Father, Prince of Peace" (Isa. 9:6).

If the nativity celebrates a child born in human flesh and bearing the name of God, then Epiphany is about our recognition of that mystery. The great epiphany—the "aha" that captured the imagination of the early church—is the act of seeing the incarnation more clearly.

Such recognitions don't come easily. Even after eight years of theological studies, I understood this familiar word *incarnation* only as an abstract theological proposition. It wasn't until recent years that my deeper engagement with the incarnation—my own epiphany of sorts—profoundly shifted my understanding of the Christian message away from abstraction and toward embodied presence. What God reveals in the nativity is not a proposition but a word made flesh, a response to the most pressing questions of human life—which are not "Does God exist?" or "Who is God?" but rather "Who am I?" and "Do I belong?" and "What is the meaning of my life?"

The incarnation is, of course, a revelation of who God is and what God is like; but it is also a revelation of who we are as human beings and of God's posture toward us. By taking on flesh and engaging the ordinary, God binds himself to the creation and affirms the goodness of the world he has chosen to inhabit. Realizing this can transform our sense of ourselves and our stance toward others, opening our eyes to God's presence in every aspect of this messy, fragile, and often mysterious life.

As an affirmation of the physical world, the incarnation also confronts our tendency toward dualism—the severing of the life of the spirit from the life of the flesh. The first letter to Timothy reminds us that legalism is almost always the result of such dualistic thinking. But the incarnation reveals an indelible connection between the spiritual and the physical; Paul can assert the goodness of all of creation because Christ has fully participated in and embraced the life of this world.

And herein lies the epiphany of this season. Unto us a child is born who restores our wholeness by re-ligamenting (the root meaning of religion) the spiritual with the physical world, bringing it together in wholeness. This revelation of divine presence among us, infusing even the most mundane aspects of life, renews our sense of belonging in this world and strengthens our bonds to creation and to each other, as co-bearers of the incarnate presence of God.

Lord we are awake to the wonder of the miracle—
that you loved us so much you have entered, endured,
and sacrificed for our wholeness and completeness.
You call us to live out the new creation we are
called to be. Give us courageous, thankful,
and wonder-filled lives, we pray. Amen.

Greg Pennoyer is the executive director of the Humanitas Group in Vancouver, British Columbia, where he lives.

About the Paintings

About the Paintings

Fr. Rick Ganz

The Adoration of the Shepherds (see front and back cover)
by Rembrandt Harmenszoon van Rijn (1606–1669)

Rembrandt was born and lived in the Netherlands. His intensely realistic portrayal of people—ugly with no glamour—places the divine mystery, and gift, where we do not expect perfection to be offered. This is a painting of Luke 2:15–20.

To notice: (1) Jesus is the light—the light of the world—in this stable at night, the presence of which light draws our eye, and holds it, proving that we are made for the light, that we can't resist looking where the light is; (2) The dog appears to be looking at us with a skeptical face; he is on guard, ready to jump us if we threaten in some way the child and his family.

[Rembrandt Harmensz. van Rijn, The Adoration of the Shepherds, 1646, Oil on canvas, 65 x 55 cm. National Gallery, London.]

The Visitation (see page 1)
by Ludovico Brea (1450–1522/23)

Brea was a painter from Genoa, Italy. He painted this oil on wood, and it is found in the Convent of St. Dominic in Taggia, Italy. Taggia is located halfway between Genoa, Italy, and Nice, France, on the coast road. This is a painting of Luke 1:39–45.

To notice: (1) The crossing of the arms and hands of the two women, which may indicate the joining in friendship of the Old Testament (John the Baptist in Elizabeth's womb) and the New Testament (Jesus in the womb of Mary); (2) Who is the man standing in the door behind Mary—Joseph, husband of Mary, or Zechariah, husband of Elizabeth?

[Ludovico Brea, The Visitation, 1512–1513, Oil on wood, Convento di San Domenico, Taggia, Italy.]

Arrival of the Holy Family in Front of the Inn at Bethlehem (see page 21)

by Joseph von Fuehrich (1800–1876)

Fuehrich was an Austrian painter, who eventually taught in Vienna. In Vienna, he was a member of the Nazarene association of young artists, a protest movement in Europe that sought to restore the centrality of the religious and moral purpose of painting for the service of culture and to return to a medieval style of painting. This is a painting of Luke 2:7.

To notice: (1) The irritated look on the donkey's face, ears back—it knows that something is not right; (2) Mary's hands joined, a sign of the peaceful joining of heaven and earth, while the other two hands of Joseph and the innkeeper symbolize conflict—one pointing toward the entrance; the other pointing away to the open road.

[Joseph von Fuehrich, Arrival of the Holy Family in Front of the Inn at Bethlehem, 1838, Oil on canvas, 35 x 44.2 cm. Nationalgalerie, Staatliche Museen, Berlin, Germany.]

The Adoration of the Magi (see page 41)

by Francesco da Ponte Bassano The Younger (1559–1592)

Bassano is the name of the town—Bassano del Grappa, Italy, located northwest of Venice, and halfway to Verona—where Bassano was born as the eldest son of a famous family of painters—the da Ponte family. He took his life at the age of thirty-three right after the death of his father, Jacopo. This is a painting of Matthew 2:1–12.

To notice: (1) The impossible proximity of an ancient Greek and partially shattered column and the humble stable of Bethlehem; (2) The two sources of light in the painting.

[Francesco da Ponte Bassano The Younger, The Adoration of the Magi, 1585–1590, Oil on canvas, 121 x 128 cm. Kunsthistorisches Museum, Vienna, Austria.]

The Annunciation to the Shepherds (see page 61)

by Benjamin Gerritsz Cuyp (1612–1652)

Cuyp was a Dutch painter, born in the Netherlands, whose work shows the influence of his contemporary Dutchman Rembrandt van Rijn (1606–1669) when he paints a dark, lightless boundary in the center of which he pulls out a scene of light and definition. This is a painting of Luke 2:8–14.

To notice: (1) The outspread arms of five of the shepherds in imitation of the gesture of the visiting angel; (2) The staircase of wood in possible reference to Jacob's ladder in Genesis 28:12.

[Benjamin Gerritsz Cuyp, The Annunciation to the Shepherds, c. 1612–1652, Oil on canvas, 101 x 99.5 cm. Hermitage Museum, Saint Petersburg, Russia.]

The Adoration of the Shepherds (see page 81)
by Lorenzo Lotto (1480–1556)

Lotto was born in Venice, Italy, and his style is especially known as a successful blending of Venetian and Middle Italian styles of that period under the significant influence of Raphael (1483–1520) in Rome. This is a painting of Luke 2:15–20.

To notice: (1) The angels who announced the tidings of great joy to the shepherds, not only announced this news but then escorted the shepherds to the stable; (2) It would be exceedingly difficult not to pay attention to the presence of two angels in the room, yet Mary only has eyes for her son.

[Lorenzo Lotto, The Adoration of the Shepherds, 1534, Oil on canvas, 147 x 166 cm. Musei Civici d'Arte e Storia, Brescia.]

The Flight into Egypt (see page 89)
by Juan Rodriguez Juarez (1657–1728)

Juarez came from a distinguished family of portrait painters of Spain, in the Baroque style, but who lived in New Spain (which was renamed Mexico in 1821). This is a painting of Matthew 2:13–15.

To notice: (1) The unexpected serenity, and normalcy, of the holy family who had to leave everything in flight from a murdering Herod (Matthew 2:16–18), perhaps because they were led there by two angels; (2) The only character looking at us is the donkey.

[Juan Rodriguez Juarez, The Flight into Egypt, c1720, Oil on canvas, 109 x 213 cm. Queretaro Museum, Mexico.]

The Light of the World (see page 125)
by William Holman Hunt (1827–1910)

Hunt was born and lived in London, eventually helping found in 1848 the pre-Raphaelite Brotherhood of English painters and poets, who were committed to a closer and more rich observation of the natural world—not the idea of a tree, for example, but what an actual and particular tree uniquely presents to view. This is a painting of Revelation 3:20–21.

To notice: (1) The risen Christ, but still wearing the crown of thorns, approaches at night to knock on a long-unopened door that is overgrown with vines—how did he find such a hidden door and then knock there?; (2) Why is Jesus looking at us rather than at the door, and whoever is behind that door?

[William Holman Hunt, The Light of the World, 1851–1853, Oil on canvas, 59.8 x 125.5 cm. Keble College, Oxford, United Kingdom.]

Notes

1. John Barton and John Muddiman, "Romans 3," *The Oxford Bible Commentary* (Oxford: Oxford University Press, 2001), 1092.
2. Karl Barth, trans. by Edwyn Hoskyns, *The Epistle to the Romans* (London: Oxford University Press, 1968), 151.
3. Phillips Brooks, "O Little Town of Bethlehem."
4. C. S. Lewis, *Letters to Malcolm, Chiefly on Prayer: Reflections on the Intimate Dialogue between Man and God* (New York: Harvest Harcourt Books, 1964), 23.
5. Dallas Willard, *The Spirit of Disciplines: Understanding How God Changes Lives* (New York: HarperOne, 1999), 120.
6. Abraham Joshua Heschel, *The Sabbath* (New York: Farrar, Straus and Giroux, 2005), 3.
7. Ibid.
8. Ibid., 18.
9. Christian Wiman, *My Bright Abyss: Meditations of a Modern Believer* (New York: Farrar, Straus and Giroux, 2013), 99.
10. Quote by George Basil Hume. (Collection of unpublished quotes, Kevin Nichols.)

MJM Grantees

4word • Adventist World Aviation • Africa New Life Ministries International • Aglow International • Agros International • Alaska Christian College • Alaska Pacific University • Aldersgate Conference Center • All God's Children International • Alpha North America • Amerson Music Ministries • Anchorage Christian Schools • Arctic Barnabas • Arctic Broadcasting • Arrow Leadership • Association of Christian Schools International • Bakke Graduate University • Barnabas Family Ministries • Beartooth Mountain Christian Ranch • Black Lake Bible Camp • Blanchet Catholic School • Boise Rescue Mission • Breakthrough Partners • Bridge Builders International • Brother Francis Shelter Kodiak • C3 Leaders • Calvary's Northern Lights Mission • Calvin College • Camp Bethel • Camp Bighorn • Camp Lutherwood • Camp Spalding • Camp Tapawingo • Canadian Inter-Varsity Christian Fellowship • Cannon Beach Conference Center • Capitol Ministries • Care Net • Carroll College • Cascades Camp • Catholic Broadcasting Northwest • Catholic Charities • Catholic Social Services Center • Cedar Springs Camp • Center for Religious Humanism • Center for Transforming Mission • Central Catholic High School • Christ Clinic • Christian College Coalition • Christian International Scholarship Foundation • Christian Media Ministries • Christian Schools International • Christianity Today International • Church Initiative • Clydehurst Christian Ranch • College of Idaho • Community Leadership Development • Community Pregnancy Clinic • Compass Center • Concordia University • Congregations for the Homeless • Council for Christian Colleges & Universities • Covenant House Alaska • Crisis Pregnancy Centers • CRISTA Ministries • Cup of Cool Water • De La Salle North Catholic High School • Dinner & A Movie • Eagle Wings Ministries • Earl Palmer Ministries • East West Ministries International • Eastern Oregon Mission • Ecumenical Ministries of Oregon • Eugene Bible College • Faithful Friends • Family Renewal Shelter • Fellowship Foundation • Fellowship of Christian Athletes • Fir Point Bible Camp • Firm Foundation School • Flathead Lutheran Bible Camp • Flying H Youth Ranch • Flying Mission USA • Focus on the Family • Forward Edge International • Friends of Menucha • Friends of the Family Ministries • Friendship House • Fruitland Bible Camp • Fuller Theological Seminary • Genesis Institute • George Fox University • Girl Scouts • Gonzaga University • Gordon College • Gospel Missionary Union • Grace Christian School • Habitat for Humanity • Haller Lake Christian Health Clinic • Helping Hands • Holy Name School • Hope in Christ Ministries • Housing Hope • Immaculate Conception School • Immaculate Heart Retreat Center • INN University Ministries • International Christian Communications • International Justice Mission • InterVarsity Christian Fellowship - USA • Jesuit High School • Jesuit Volunteer Corps • Jonah Ministries • Jubilee Reach • Kittitas County Chaplaincy • KLEOS Ministries • Kodiak Baptist Mission • Krista Foundation for Global Citizenship • Leadership Catalyst • Life Services • Light Side • Lighthouse Christian Ministries • LINC Ministries • Luis Palau Association • Lutheran Family Services • Lutheran Outdoor Ministries • MarriageTeam • Medical Teams International • Mending the Soul Ministries • Mending Wings • Mercy Corps • Mike Silva Evangelism • Military Community Youth Ministries • Ministry Coaching International • Missoula 3:16 • Montana Bible College • Montana Rescue Mission • Multnomah University • My Father's House • Nehemiah Ministries • New Earth/Tierra Nueva • New Horizons Ministries • New Tribes Mission • North Park University • Northern Light Network • Northwest Baptist Seminary • Northwest Christian College • Northwest Family Services • Northwest Leadership Foundation • Northwest Nazarene University • Northwest University • Open Arms International • Open House • Operation Nightwatch • Oregon Episcopal School • Oregon Leadership Development Institute • Our Lady of Lourdes School • Our Lady of the Rosary • Pacific Association for Theological Studies • Pacific Lutheran University • Parachute Ministries • Partners International • Peace Community Center • Peacemaker Ministries • Peak 7 Adventures • Portland Christian Schools • Portland Leadership Foundation • Portland Lutheran School • Portland Rescue Mission • Poverello Center • Pregnancy Resource Centers • Pro Athletes Outreach • Project PATCH • Puget Sound Christian Clinic • Q Place • Raphael House • Re:source Global • REACH • Reach Out & Care Wheels • Regent College • Reid Saunders Association • Rescue Missions of the Northwest • Responder Life • Rocky Mountain Bible Mission • Safe Place Ministries • Saint Martin's University • Salem Free Medical Clinic • Salem Leadership Foundation • Salvation Army in the Northwest • Search Ministries • Seattle Association for Theological Education • Seattle Pacific University • Seattle School of Theology and Psychology • Seattle University • SEND International • Silver Lake Camp • Society of St. Vincent de Paul • SonBridge Community Center • Sonshine Bible Clubs • Special K Ranch, Inc. • St. Martin's College • St. Stephen's Academy • St. Vincent de Paul • Stillwater Youth Center • Sunnyside Counseling Center • Tacoma Rescue Mission • Tacoma-Pierce County Chaplaincy • Tape Ministries Northwest • Taproot Theatre • Teen Challenge International • The Grotto • The Navigators • The Seattle School for Psychology and Theology • To Shine Too • Transitional Youth • Trinity Western University • Trout Creek Bible Camp, Inc. • Twin Rocks Friends Conference Association • Union Gospel Missions • United Indian Missions • University of Portland • Urban Impact • Veritas Forum • Victory Ministries • Vine Maple Place • Vision House • Voice for Christ Ministries • Walla Walla University • Warm Beach Christian Camps • Warner Pacific College • WAY Media • Wellspring Revival Ministries • West Hills Christian School • Western Conservative Baptist Seminary • Western Seminary • Westside Christian High School • Whitworth University • Wiconi International • Wild Canyon Events • Windrider Institute • Wings of Hope • World Vision • Wycliffe Bible Translators • Yellowstone Baptist College • Yellowstone Boys and Girls Ranch • YMCA of the Northwest • Young Life • You're Not Alone • Youth Dynamics • Youth for Christ • Youth Transition Network • YWCA of the Northwest